Praise for

"These pages offer the voice of a writer of modern sensibility who dares to leap across time and space to unveil the true nature of soul. Rarely does a memoir have such power and beauty to awaken our own souls in daily life. Read this book!"

—Christina Donnell, PhD, author of
*Transcendent Dreaming: Stepping into Our Human Potential*

"This is a book about deep living—a book about courage, searching, finding and telling the truth. It shows the rest of us how we, too, can mine the depths of our lives to find what we are really looking for in order to live an authentic, meaningful, and flourishing life."

—Henry Emmons, MD
Integrative Psychiatrist and author of *The Chemistry of Joy:
A Three-Step Program for Overcoming Depression through
Western Science and Eastern Wisdom* and *The Chemistry of
Calm: A Powerful, Drug-Free Plan to Quiet Your Fears and
Overcome Your Anxiety*

"In this engaging, insightful memoir, Keri Mangis shares her deep wisdom about the journeys we embark on with each human incarnation, and the soul purpose behind all we experience in our 'skins,' or bodies. Through her highly relatable heroine Sëri, in collaboration with Sëri's soul friend Rasa, Keri unfolds one woman's tale of discovering the Great Truth of our lives and the loving purpose for all that we undergo on earth. Ultimately, she shows us how to discover joy. For readers seeking inspirational knowledge about their higher purpose, their soul guides, and the lessons of every life, *Embodying Soul* is a marvelous, heart-opening excursion."

—Christine Warren, teacher and author of
*Navigating Change: Conscious Endings, Visionary Beginnings*

"New stories are coming through to heal our collective imagination. Keri Mangis's *Embodying Soul* belongs to this emergent art form. Through the lens of her own life story, told with vulnerability, humor, and grace, Mangis invites us into a world where the rich inner landscape of the psyche is always speaking, always full of gifts for us. We receive these gifts—of curiosity unleashed, self-mothering, inner re-wilding—and are set free of the old limits on our imaginations. Be ready, dear reader: adventuring into this book may change you. You may become more aware of the inner conversation between your emotions or begin listening for the voice of your soul, or simply forgive yourself for the times you haven't listened. And you may remember another gleaming facet of who you came here to be."

—Opal C McCarthy
Author of the poetry collection *SURGE*

"Keri Mangis has written a book to be savored over a cup of herbal tea; shared with friends; and, once completed, kept nearby for further reference. Part autobiography, part self-help, part soul-realm imagination, it is a flowing stream of gathering awareness revealing a story many of us can relate to. Each of the major emotions becomes a companion along the way, not just an affliction to be ignored, shoved aside, or belittled. And Mangis's inventive, engaging style promises humor, depth, drama, comedy, humility, and profound humanity. This is an excellent book."

—Ronald E. Moor
Healer, teacher, and spiritual guide

*Embodying Soul*, a courageous piece of work, speaks to the beauty and pain of the human condition. Keri Mangis captivates the reader with her vulnerability, creativity, and insight, inspiring us to explore the true depth of our souls to better understand ourselves and one another. This book is sure to infuse more purpose and meaning into your life."

—Julie Burton, author of
*The Self-Care Solution: A Modern Mother's Must-Have Guide to Health and Well-Being* and
Founder of ModernWell

"From separation of self to the reclamation of soul, this book is a fascinating sojourn into one woman's life process. Courageously shared, her journey will inspire the reader's own soul awareness."

—Carol J. Murto
Author of *Soul Awareness: A Spiritual Awakening to Self-Knowledge and Healing*

"A beautifully interwoven tale of the human-soul experience as seen from both sides. Keri's honest recounting of her path to embodiment lends courage to anyone who longs to reclaim emotional wisdom and answer the authentic call of endless curiosity."

—Amy Hallberg, author of
*German Awakening: Tales of an American Life*, Certified
Master Coach, and founder of Courageous Wordsmith

"The courage of Keri Mangis to engage in a public dialogue with her soul is a feat not to be taken lightly, for her book *Embodying Soul* will shape how we all communicate with ourselves and rediscover the truth of our souls."

—Tim Miejan
Editor and publisher of *The Edge* magazine

"While reading this story, rendered with honesty and grit, I couldn't help but reflect on my own emotional landscape with new understanding. And I was moved by the entertaining and enlightening view of what the soul realm might be like. A cathartic book, to be sure, and a must-read for those on the path of transformation!"

—Tara Cindy Sherman
Tree Spirit Yoga founder, Yoga Alliance Continued
Education Provider, and Registered Yoga Teacher

"The author's principal goal is to inform, and the book becomes a kind of self-help guide that encourages intuition, communication, and letting go. A nontraditional but effective memoir about one woman's discovery of spiritualism."

—*Kirkus Reviews*

"Have you ever thought about contacting your soul? Well, this memoir might help you do it.…The book is profound and will help readers look at life with a different perspective and work toward being in alignment with their life, embodying characteristics like softness, calmness, approachability, courage, humility, patience, and strength."

—Mamta Mahavan
Reviewer, Readers' Favorite

"This book gave me better clarity on my own past behavior, current life choices, and future endeavors. It's a gift to escape into another's story while also gaining greater understanding of your own! I will read this book again (and again) and know that each time it will unveil even more."

—Heather Corndorf
mXe founder and movement specialist

# EMBODYING SOUL

*I am not this hair,*
*I am not this skin,*
*I am the soul that lives within.*

—RUMI

# EMBODYING
# SOUL

## A RETURN TO WHOLENESS

# KERI MANGIS

*a memoir of new beginnings*

May endless
curiosity always win
the day!

Keri

**CURIOSA**
PUBLISHING
MINNEAPOLIS, MINNESOTA

*Published by*

Curiosa Publishing
3109 West 50th Street, PMB #135
Minneapolis, MN 55410
www.curiosapublishing.com

Editor: Ellen Kleiner
Book design and production: Angela Werneke
Cover art: Dee Gieser

First Edition

*Embodying Soul* is factually accurate, except that names, locales, and individual traits have been altered to preserve coherence while protecting privacy.

Printed in Canada

PUBLISHER'S CATALOGING-IN-PUBLICATION DATA

Names: Mangis, Keri, author.

Title: Embodying soul: a return to wholeness : a memoir of new beginnings / Keri Mangis.

Description: First edition. | Minneapolis, Minnesota : Curiosa Publishing, [2020]

Identifiers: ISBN: 9781732991200 (paperback) | 9781732991217 (ebook) | LCCN: 2018914551

Subjects: LCSH: Mind and body. | Soul. | Reincarnation. | Self-actualization (Psychology) | Ego (Psychology) | Curiosity—Psychological aspects. | Mental health. | Emotions. | Autobiography. | LCGFT: Autobiographies. | BISAC: PHILOSOPHY / Mind & Body. | SELF-HELP / Personal Growth / General. | BIOGRAPHY & AUTOBIOGRAPHY / Personal Memoirs.

Classification: LCC: BF637.S4 M36 2020 | DDC: 158.1--dc23

1   3   5   7   9   10   8   6   4   2

To my dearest daughters, Cameron and Kelsey ~

May you both flourish in endless curiosity

as you continue to choose your own life adventures

## ACKNOWLEDGMENTS

WHILE THE PROCESS OF WRITING THIS BOOK was often a solitary one, it was never done alone. Thank you to Opal McCarthy for encouraging me to write stories from the truest place within myself, my soul.

Thank you to editor Jane Usher and her wise soul, Lady Jane, who, from the very beginning, loved the book's characters, especially Endless Curiosity; due to her belief in the magic I wanted to weave, the Soul Realm rained down its stories and knowledge.

Thank you to my friend and spiritual guide Christina Donnell, who saw the sudden quiet and solitude in my life as the blessing it was and pointed me straight into this void, from which my book was birthed.

Thank you to Cindy Seelen, Terry Jo Alfred, Amy Hallberg, Mary Berg, and Elizabeth Jarrett Andrew, who read early drafts and offered valuable insights.

Thank you to my mom, who read several drafts, repeatedly reminding me not to worry about revealing our personal stories in violation of the stoic silence for which our Scandinavian blood stands, and whose love and unconditional support gave me the courage to publish like no courage I could've summoned from within.

Thank you to my dad for loving me unconditionally and for all the advice over the years, taken or not.

Thank you to my many teachers, guides, healers, and fellow spiritual travelers for listening to and loving me back to wholeness. Though only a few made it into this book as characters, many more helped me grow my voice and power.

Thank you to all my yoga students, fellow yoga teachers, and Ayurvedic friends and clients for trusting me while I walked many windy paths and for letting me go with grace when it was time; you are family to me.

Thank you to Julie Burton and Nina Sackheim Badzin, as well as to all members of the ModernWell Writing Studio, for offering your honest feedback, support, and encouragement.

Thank you to Ellen Kleiner of Blessingway Authors' Services for tending carefully to every word of this story, for walking Endless Curiosity and me through our many questions, and for encouraging and guiding me to slip on yet another new and exciting skin, that of self-publisher.

Finally, a special thank you to Todd, my supportive and adoring husband, who, when warned about intimate details I intended to share with the world, would shrug and say, "Well, it's the truth," and who, except for complaining that I no longer did my share of the yardwork, never failed to help me find the time and energy needed to complete this book.

∽

# CONTENTS

# Family Flags

"LET'S BEGIN TODAY BY GOING BACK TO YOUR CHILDHOOD. What would you say were your family's core values?" asked my rosy-cheeked, spiky-haired, middle-aged therapist while holding a ballpoint pen an inch away from her yellow legal pad, ready to scribble my family wisdom. Her office, tucked in a basement in a suburb of Minneapolis, was comfortable and quiet. On the wall behind her were several framed diplomas and on the wall to my right some abstract art, but the wall to my left, where a clock should've been to ensure clients didn't overstay their sessions, was blank—like my mind.

With a mug of steaming peppermint tea cupped in my hands intended to calm me, I considered what my childhood could have had to do with my current anxiety. I'd already had a few appointments with this therapist during which we'd concentrated on the impact of anxiety on my life. I had told her about the emptiness I felt, my mind's lack of clarity, my trembling body. I had explained how the anxiety also made me feel cold, even while sweating across my lower back and under my arms enough to soak through my clothing. I had revealed that nevertheless most people never suspected my inner turmoil, because I hid my true feelings under layers of self-discipline.

She had asked me what situations triggered my anxiety,

and I had identified the group settings where participants had to share something personal, like my yoga classes, workshops, or trainings. I explained that when teaching yoga, a group setting where I was in control of the agenda, I rarely experienced anxiety unless it was the first day of a new class, and that, once I got to know my students, no one guessed that I suffered from anxiety. So, I had told her, when some occasion triggered anxiety I just waited for it to dissipate. Teaching yoga, I explained, was a calling that made me feel more whole and alive than in any other area of my life, and I would not, could not, give it up.

She had listened to my revelations and called my anxiety "social" anxiety, though I would have called it "lack of control" anxiety. She had then asked what calming techniques I'd tried. I explained that although I knew all kinds of breathing techniques and positive visualizations and affirmations, in moments of debilitating anxiety nothing worked and all I could do was wait for the situation that had triggered it to end and my body to return to normal. Those had been embarrassing admissions of weakness, but the questions about my feelings of anxiety had made sense so I'd answered them honestly.

But now she was probing into my childhood, which did not seem to honor the urgency of my situation: I was thirty-four years old and married; had two children, both colicky as babies; had spent the last six months battling my fourth case of hives, necessitating my first emergency room visit and a steroid prescription; the yoga classes I was teaching were on hold due to my illness; my marriage was on the verge of failure; and when I had finally felt strong enough to leave the sanctuary of my darkened bedroom to drive to Blockbuster to rent a movie, the energy required to engage in retail pleasantries had exhausted me so much I had gone home and fallen asleep, no longer interested in a movie. And here my therapist was inquiring about my long-ago childhood. What did she want to know—the kind of cake that had been served on my fourth birthday? I wondered, sarcastically.

In an attempt to avoid encouraging what I considered my therapist's nonrelevant rerouting, I bit my lip and said, "I'm sorry, I don't really understand."

"Many families have sayings that bond them, like 'We all stand together' or 'Blood is thicker than water,'" she explained patiently.

"Not mine," I asserted, a little defensively, then gave an apologetic shrug.

"Well, let me ask this: Did you receive any kind of verbal instruction about your family identity or how to present yourself in the world?" said my therapist.

Suddenly, a memory formed in my mind like a single raindrop, and I revealed, "When my brothers and I asked my dad what he wanted for Christmas, he always said, 'Good kids.'"

"Okay, and what did that mean to you?" she inquired, encouragingly.

I dropped my head, expecting a protective curtain of long, brown hair to fall around my face, forgetting that I'd recently had it cut short, and replied, "Follow rules, don't cause trouble, stay out of the way. It was just a joke, though. We usually got him socks or something."

"Were you the kind of kid to cause trouble?" she then asked, pressing me further.

I sniggered and answered, "Hardly. Goody-Two-Shoes is more like it." My self-loathing released a stream of something like endorphins through my body, which felt good, like a smoker taking a long-awaited drag on a cigarette. At least it felt better than being confused and vulnerable.

"Any other instructions or mottoes from home?" she inquired, smiling, her cheeks forming small apples beneath her eyes.

The fact that she wasn't letting this probing go made me suspect I was failing to adequately answer what must've been to her a straightforward question. I felt anxious, imagining her other clients rattling off family mottoes. I set the tea on a coaster on the polished glass table before me, rolled my eyes upward, and strained to hear some other slogan, statement, or manifesto from my childhood inside the cavern of my mind. But all I heard was the North Dakota wind howling.

"I can't think of anything else," I said, attempting a tone of finality.

"Well," she continued, unfazed, "think of it another way. If your family had had a flag flying outside your house, what would it have said?"

I stifled a chuckle. A flag flying outside our house? We never would have let ourselves be so visible. We were a quiet family living a simple, frugal life, with a sense of duty and pride—not an outer pride of flag-flying but an inner pride that worked like an invisible rubber band of resilience, helping us snap back into shape when the world's cares pulled on us—except for me, apparently. I wondered what my family would think if they knew I was seeking help from a shrink just to get by day to day and paying for it with hard-earned money, not even my money but my husband's money, since my little hobby of a yoga business didn't pay the bills and my business degree was sitting in a drawer turning yellow rather than proudly displayed on a wall like my therapist's degrees. My parents wouldn't have had time for such psychobabble but would have persevered through any pain, if indeed they had been forced to recognize it.

I considered the two choices I saw before me: A) tell my therapist what I thought about her nosy, irrelevant question, storm out, and never return, or B) tell her nothing about my discomfort, grit my teeth, and muster up a good enough answer to her searching question, as championed by family habits. I knew that option A was not a viable option; at the time, showing frustration or confusion was to me synonymous with admitting weakness, which I felt would leave me dangerously vulnerable.

"Do what you have to do now, you can panic later," my mom had always said, even though I never really saw her panic later. I only heard her crying once, quietly, as I listened at her bedroom door and knew better than to ask her about it, then or later. From her, I had learned that dwelling on emotions, or "complaining," solved nothing, pulled energy away from urgent daily tasks, and took the focus away from building a good reputation.

So option B was what I took. Like opening up a family

album that had been tucked away in a closet for years, I creaked open my memories of childhood, figuring that my therapist would soon see that my ancient past had little relevance to my present concerns, and then we could begin addressing my anxiety or, if not, I could simply stop making appointments and move on with my life. What I didn't see at the time was how certain family behaviors would turn out to be red flags, revealing internal barriers I would need to surmount before forging an inclusive and loving relationship with my emotions and myself—the very definition of embodying one's soul and a potent beginning for a return to wholeness.

# PART I

## First Line of Defense

❧

*Human skin is the first line of defense*
*against the dangers of the outside world,*
*shielding us from disease-causing agents and the*
*injuries that can occur through daily living.*
*Also thanks to our skin our messy interior—*
*our emotions—*
*can remain safely hidden from view.*

## CHAPTER 1

## *Travel Suitcase*

I FEEL LIKE I AM FLOATING IN A VOID of blissful amnesia, not yet knowing who or where I am. Out of habit, I pull my lungs toward the center of my body to draw a breath, but find it is unnecessary. The energy swirls in and out of me effortlessly.

To my left is a field shrouded in darkness, outlined by only the light of the distant stars but pulsing with life like a seeded spring garden. To my right is the outline of a settee for two, woven from the branches and twigs of a giant redwood tree magically braided into vine and floral patterns that form its seat and back. A gentle breeze carries its fragrant scent my way, which soothes and settles me.

My surroundings begin to feel more familiar. I emerge from the ether of obscurity aware now that I am in the Soul Realm, the space to which every soul returns between human incarnations to experience needed healing, reflection, and guidance.

A suitcase materializes from the void and floats down onto the settee. It is a hard-shell one, dandelion yellow, with a smooth, glossy covering adorned with tiny stuffed bears, freshly painted in luminescent pastels. One bear has a rainbow stitched across its belly, another has a heart, and a third holds flowers in its furry blue fingers. Intuitively I know this is my suitcase for my journey to the Earth Realm. I locate a metal latch on the suitcase, flip it up, peer inside, and see that it is empty except for memories, which waft out, one after another, the enticing aroma of cotton, sea air, fresh coconut milk, and ripe papaya.

With the appearance of my travel suitcase, I remember how the Soul Realm is like a well-organized airport where, having just gotten off one flight, souls can choose where to venture next. But unlike in an airport no soul is subject to a predetermined schedule before its next journey to the Earth Realm. Should I choose to leave, I will first pack my suitcase with special tools found only in the Soul Realm that are essential to creating a fully conscious embodiment in which I am able to experience the wholeness of human life in the Earth Realm.

While I wait, my silhouette begins to closely resemble inhabitants of the Earth Realm as the Age of Pisces gives way to the Age of Aquarius—a time of great possibility and momentous change for the world. Soon I take on what might be a vaguely female shape that sways with swaths of fire and smoke. Whether these are the remaining embers of my most recent past life, the first sparks of my future life, or a little of both, I cannot say.

Though I have form, I do not yet have substance. But it may not be long before I am once again wrapped inside the confines of human skins—both the physical skin, with its many miraculous functions for the human body that permit protection, growth, absorption, excretion, regulation, and sensation, and the metaphorical skins of roles, duties, and titles. The value of human skins is unmeasurable for souls who wish to expand their consciousness beyond the familiar in the Earth Realm by trying something new. Some humans find their skins protective, especially while risking exposure to the unknown; others find their skins constricting and feel like imposters when performing behaviors associated with them. But whether humans feel an attachment or aversion to their many skins, only when they learn to move through them with the fluidity of a snake will they come to know the freedom, peace, and joy that is their birthright.

Pondering my decision whether or not to leave, I run my fingers gently along the rim of the suitcase where my name is embossed in tiny letters: Serene Voyager, the name with which the constellations serenade me, given to me to reflect my love of adventure and observant yet calm perspective, both useful qualities in the shifting landscape of the Earth Realm. Here in the Soul Realm, though, I go simply by Sëri.

## CHAPTER 2

# Breaking Out of Identity Confinement

DURING MY CHILDHOOD, THE CONFINING NATURE of my midwestern conservative roots tangled with my pursuit of adventure and natural tendency toward curiosity about the unknown. I was born in Fargo, North Dakota, in June 1972, the oldest of three siblings and the only girl. Growing up, Tim and Terry, two and eight years younger, respectively, and I always had a warm house to come home to after school, food on the table every night, new clothes every fall, and stockings full of presents at Christmas. Our family owned a lake cabin, where we learned to water ski and enjoyed evening camp-fires. We took family road trips around the country, and had plenty of family and friends to gather with on weekends and holidays.

The worst thing about my earliest years was disliking my younger brother Tim, though a recurring dream helped me keep him in his place. In the dream, a witch would pop up from be-hind my bed in our shared bedroom, I'd call my brother over, we'd gape at the witch, unsure of what she might do to us. She'd give us a lecture—I don't remember about what—and then offer me a piece of hard candy and hit Tim over the head with a mallet before disappearing back behind the bed. It was a satisfying dream.

My dad was born and raised in a small city about an hour west of Fargo with three siblings, two older and one younger. My mom was born and raised on a farm about an hour south of Fargo with four siblings, one older and three younger. He a city boy and she a country girl, they met when she was going to nursing school in his city, where he was working as a grocer while attending college. They married when he was twenty and she was nineteen. I was born two years later.

Except for some apartment-hopping around eastern North Dakota when I was a baby, we made only one big move as a family: to West Fargo, where my parents had purchased a house when I was five. I remember seeing it for the first time, studying the simple yellow three-bedroom, one-level house from the window of the car, and feeling excitement about finally getting a bedroom—and my candy-giving witch—all to myself.

Remaining at this house while all three of us kids grew up and eventually graduated from the same high school was an intentional decision by my dad, in contrast to how he had been raised. My dad's dad had been a school superintendent and a strict, demanding parent with a habit of drinking on the job, resulting in my dad's family being forced to move at least seven times during his school years to various small towns in central North Dakota. In rural North Dakota in the 1950s and 1960s, his family had been able to move quietly from town to town without his dad's reputation following them. I can still hear pain in his voice when we talk about what it was like for him as a child to move to a place where he had no friends, where he was both the new kid and the superintendent's kid. So my dad promised he would not drag us around, a promise he kept, even when it meant turning down better jobs, raises, or fancier titles, giving us kids the opportunity to sink roots into Fargo's soil. I appreciated his sacrifice of opportunities to provide us with a stable home environment.

My dad was in the car business. Though he worked in finance and insurance departments rather than sales, he took the stereotype of the crooked car salesman personally, and, as if to correct his own karma, was determined to build a positive reputation in Fargo. While I don't remember my dad sitting us down to purposely teach us that a reputation is earned not given, we learned this through observing him. To this day, my dad, though retired, maintains his positive reputation among locals where he now lives with my mom, just across the North Dakota state line in Minnesota.

Growing up, I could initially see the virtue of staying in one place to build a reputation as it gave my dad a sense of security and belonging. Soon, however, building a reputation felt too much like erecting walls of identity confinement. I realized that in the fairly small town of Fargo, once people had a belief about who you were it was difficult to become anything else. Once you were an athlete, you were supposed to remain an athlete. If you were funny, you were expected to find humor in every situation. And if you were known as a good girl you had to stay that way, even when you really wanted to party or be asked out by a notoriously bad boy.

So my dad's early life seemed almost romantic to me—minus the part related to his dad's alcohol abuse. I was attracted to the idea of slipping from town to town under the cover of night, showing up in a place where no one would know anything about me or attempt to force me to conform to some prescribed role or path. Then, just about the time people would inevitably start to label me as this or that, I could head off to a new town, as if slipping into a new skin.

Thus at age twenty, the age my parents were when they settled down to raise a family, I said good-bye to my family and friends and moved away from Fargo, intent on seeking adventure and following dreams.

## CHAPTER 3

## *The River of Forgetting*

I GAZE OUT TO THE HORIZON, where a first ribbon of pink and turquoise light appears, dispelling the darkness and inviting me to explore my surroundings. Lilies, orchids, lotuses, and marigolds, sparkling like fireflies, now grow in the once-empty field on my left. As I walk, the terrain shifts from rocky to pebbly to sandy. Suddenly, I hear water rushing below. I look down and gasp, as I see that I am standing on a precipice above a rushing river. My soul body trembles. The river, which has a curvy feminine figure, winds along a narrow gulch yet is deep. The water is so pure that even from up here I see schools of pink salmon swimming upstream and downstream, assuring me that this river is no ordinary river.

I sit down on the ledge of the precipice, my legs dangling over the edge, to consider my options. Postponement of this trip is one option, and cancellation is another, both leading to no immediate negative consequences since I can remain at this level of consciousness, taking pleasure in my palpable connection with Source, for as long as I like. Yet another option is to travel through the cosmos again, staying free rather than entangling myself inside another human skin. These other choices are all far less precarious than the one indicated by the suitcase that has been presented to me.

Feeling hesitant and uncertain, I step back from the edge of the precipice.

"Yoo-hoo, Sëri! Are you here?" asks a lilting voice, as behind me a sequined, disheveled figure emerges through a sliver of light, grabbing at a flurry of papers and books whirling about her.

"Rasa! Oh, what a welcome surprise!" I exclaim as I observe my soul guide, sparking with enthusiasm, draped in exotic colors. Her presence reassures me. I help her gather up the papers and books. Once everything is safely back inside her red sequined tote bag, we embrace warmly.

"Yes, dear, it is me!" says Rasa, her boisterous laughter lightening the seriousness invoked by the precipice and the river.

"Oh, you cannot imagine the beginning I have had!" I say, relieved to be able to talk about it with my good friend and soul guide. "First, I could not remember who I was or where; next I nearly fell into the river; and then a strange, humanlike hesitation washed over me, making me wary about taking another trip to the Earth Realm."

Rasa rests a hand on my shoulder to reassure me and explains, "That was doubt you felt, a particularly human feeling. The forgetting process happened to you last time as well, though you do not remember that now." She pulls her shoulders back, indicates herself with a bejeweled hand, and says, "Meet your temporary travel guide! I have come to ensure that all your questions and concerns are addressed!"

I instantly relax as I recall that no soul embarks on a journey to the Earth Realm without the insight of another soul who can provide guidance. Without a guide like Rasa, souls would likely move through lifetimes blindly, one after another, like some human beings pass their days driven only by ingrained habit and unconscious routine. "I am most grateful for your companionship, my old friend," I say, bringing my palms together in front of my heart, "though I am curious why you have agreed to do this and what your own upcoming plans might be."

She laughs brightly and replies, "When I saw the name Serene Voyager on the list of upcoming travelers, I immediately volunteered to help you prepare for whichever trip you choose next, including the necessary packing. As for myself, I have chosen not to travel too far away from the Soul Realm for some time now as I am developing a new project, which I intend to tell you about later."

She guides me to the aromatic settee, where I sit with my legs curled comfortably while she sits regally upright, her long, thin bare feet planted firmly on the ground. She looks at me, her green eyes shimmering with love, and asks, "Do you remember that the last time I traveled to the Earth Realm it was you, Sëri, who helped me prepare and pack? This is what we soul friends do for each other."

I don't remember exactly, but it rings true that we have

helped each other numerous times during this ongoing evolution through human incarnation, offering each other whatever
is needed at various junctures of our growth. I smile into her
eyes and say, "I sense a profound fatigue, and yes, a feeling of
doubt. What I would like most is time to remember more
about who I am and, ultimately, what I need to further my own
evolving consciousness. That will help me determine where I
go next."

"Well, then, I've come well prepared," Rasa replies, wink-
ing and letting me peek at some bottles of wine, snacks, and
books tucked inside her seemingly bottomless tote bag.

I grin and reply, "Let us start with the river rushing below
the precipice. It is powerful, I remember, but the rest is foggy."

"That is the River of Forgetting, a life-altering river to be
sure, and your divinely selected path to the Earth Realm. When
you are ready, you will leap from the precipice, packed suitcase
in hand. The river will carry you, gently yet swiftly, to the
shores of the Earth Realm. As you transition from the expan-
siveness of the Soul Realm to the confinement of the Earth
Realm, the river will narrow, as will your memory of this place.
This river is so powerful and the forgetting so complete that
by the time you step out of its embrace and onto the banks of
a new life, you may even have forgotten your name. Then it will
be time to slip into an ever-changing, always-unpredictable
human skin—infant size," she explains, nudging me playfully.

"I remember the river now," I say, "but remind me why souls
must travel to the Earth Realm through the River of Forgetting. There must be wider paths that leave our memories as souls

intact. If humans remembered that their core essence is from the Soul Realm, wouldn't human life be simpler? Wouldn't their world be a wiser, more inclusive place if everyone could remember that they said yes to living in human skin with full understanding of what human life entails?"

"Oh, my dear! Those are no easy questions, though they are often the first ones on many souls' minds upon witnessing the sweeping power of the River of Forgetting. The answer is yes, there are pathways that don't result in such a complete forgetting, though they are reserved for souls who are traveling to the Earth Realm to become seers or prophets, souls who must retain more of their soul memory to do their work effectively. Your embarkation point is noted clearly as the River of Forgetting," Rasa verifies, looking in a spiral notebook. "If you wish to understand why most souls must start every life anew, imagine, for a moment, that you stand at a crossroads in human life with multiple paths before you—some of which you have traveled many times and have little left to teach you, and others that have just opened to you and are filled with abundant yet difficult challenges that could lead to increased consciousness. If you remembered all your past lives, you would already know which paths you have walked before and be able to guess at the outcomes on each one so your choices would be influenced by that information."

"Yes, I suppose it could complicate decisions. Maybe I would take a well-worn path rather than try something new. Or perhaps I might force myself down a new path, skipping a critical remaining piece on a more familiar one."

"Exactly," says Rasa, nodding. "So your decisions would be impacted by access to such memory. Souls must forget so they can play the game of life freely, without having any kind of advantage or disadvantage. But no earthly or cosmic knowledge is kept from you permanently when you seek it."

"Then the amnesia is only temporary? The River of Forgetting's effects wear off?" I ask.

"Indeed, that is the intention," my soul mate confirms.

My heart strains, as if against ropes, and I say, "I remember that confining sensation of the Earth Realm. But I also remember that this forgetting is simply a new beginning, an indication to reestablish my connection with the Soul Realm even while I remain grounded in my body in the Earth Realm."

"Yes, that is called soul embodiment, a process dependent on ego's partnership," Rasa answers. "As egos acknowledge and integrate more aspects of their souls into their lives, souls better recall their larger cosmic journey. Then, when this symbiotic relationship between soul and ego deepens, the soul more readily offers its wisdom to the ego, who can then share it with others, making the entire planet grow in consciousness and collective community. Strictly speaking," Rasa says, leaning in like she's telling me the punch line of a joke, "the soul's amnesia is only as temporary as the ego's stubbornness. You remember the ego, right?"

"How could I forget my Earth Realm bodily roommate?" I answer, chuckling.

"A roommate!" Rasa says, laughing. "Yes, that is one way to put it. But since that implies a certain cooperation, I feel it necessary to remind you about the growing obstinacy of human egos across the ages. Especially in the time and place you are set to enter, egos are far more concerned with belonging, control, safety, and success than allying themselves with their adventure-seeking souls. Many humans' egos have come to see the soul as nothing more than a literary cliché, and the soul's communication attempts as figments of their imaginations or coincidental gestures. Thus, sadly, egos often base their aspirations on promises of the Earth Realm rather than on the wisdom of their souls."

"They don't believe their souls are real," I add, remembering this challenge. "The Earth Realm has become so permeated with pretenses that few recognize truth anymore, and even fewer honor it. So they push aside their souls, not letting them take up space in the body, let alone guide life choices."

"But," Rasa says wistfully, "there are sweet, wholesome times, in childhood especially, when the ego will naturally feel the soul's love and presence. For instance, even though you will not remember yourself as soul when initially incarnated, your recent connection to the Soul Realm and its gifts, as yet unhindered by social constructs, will allow you to experience an instinctual relationship to the inhabitants and landscape of the Earth Realm."

"Oh, the joy of a human child!" I clasp my hands together, and my eyes glisten in memory.

"It is truly a special time," Rasa agrees. "But these connections will fade, sometimes gradually and other times all at once. I must remind you that this disconnection, while necessary, is a painful stage in the life of the incarnated soul. Sëri, you are right to consider the many gifts and challenges of the Earth Realm before choosing to take this trip."

"There is much to consider," I acknowledge somberly.

"But even in the midst of disconnection, your influence as a soul remains possible, and your attempts at communication may still be successful. I suggest you begin simply, like a bodily sensation for yes and another for no, and then refine your communication style as life goes on," Rasa proposes. "These seemingly small gestures can plant seeds for later, deeper connection and communication."

The signals for yes and no should be indisputable, I think. I announce, "For yes, I'll send a belly flutter that combines excitement with anticipation, along with a tingling sensation in the fingertips or across the skin, such as goose bumps or chills, and a light feeling in the heart upon occasion."

"And for no?" Rasa asks, scribbling notes in her spiral notebook.

I continue my slow walk as I consider what the signal for no ought to be then say, "Heat, because it can be adjusted from a simple blush to sweaty palms to a body rash, and additionally a heavy, constricted feeling that can easily be distinguished from the ease and lightness of yes."

"Those are unmistakable signs that even a very stubborn ego is unlikely to miss," agrees Rasa. "But know this, too: the ego must do its part by paying attention to these feelings and ultimately tracing them back to the soul. Just as it is your journey to forget and remember, it is the ego's journey as well."

I think about how what Rasa says sounds like a riddle. "So every ego must forget about the truth of the soul so that one day it can consciously choose to remember," I sum up.

"Exactly. For once she becomes aware of communication with you, that is when embodiment occurs and the journey of evolution continues," Rasa affirms.

"She?" I ask, grinning. "So my ego is a she?"

"Oops! I didn't intend to let that information slip out yet! But now that you know, congratulations—it's a girl," Rasa announces.

I sit back down to take in this news—what I had already suspected given my developing form in the Soul Realm. I have been male and female many times in my previous lives. Both genders have brought me to the state of consciousness I am at now and, in the Earth Realm, have had opportunities—some accepted, others disregarded—to make their mark on humanity. But if I am being reborn in the time and place I suspect, feminine energy will be ushering in the long-awaited transformation, influencing with gentle power rather than force. Feminine energy will be tipping hierarchies, disrupting norms, and bringing people together to change the course of humanity forever. I must be a part of that, I decide. But before it can happen I have some remembering and forgetting to do.

## CHAPTER 4

### *Forgetting Essence*

I WAS AN INQUISITIVE CHILD WHO LOVED to explore my environment, especially at my grandparents' farm, until one experience resulted in the loss of essential aspects of my adventurous self. My grandparents' farm, which included a house, a barn, and several sheds and garages, was located about an hour south of West Fargo, adjacent to the Wild Rice River and before a quiet gravel road disrupted only by an occasional whizzing car. The drivers of these cars, all of them neighbors, honked and waved, and my grandparents waved back. Out in the plains of rural North Dakota, where it could be miles between homes, neighbors didn't refer to people in terms of physical proximity but in terms of the relaxed way they related to each other, such as a pancakes-and-coffee friendliness or collective mourning at a funeral.

Until I was a teenager, I spent at least a week of each summer on the farm, in addition to the other times we visited during the year. We'd often go on Sunday afternoons in time for lunch, after which the grownups would play cards while we cousins would play outside. I would wander over to the barn to hunt for the farm cats, or peek in at the cows in their pens, or walk through my grandma's garden, studying the rows of tomatoes, carrots, lettuce, and potatoes.

Sometimes, in late summer, I'd tag along with my grandpa to combine his wheat fields. I'd stand next to him in the enclosed compartment of the combine harvester, smelling the scent of his sweat mixed with hay. Or my grandpa would let me steer the combine, sitting between his legs on the worn leather seat. We'd lumber silently down one row and up the next. Watching the wheat surrender its tall, flowing stalks to something new made my belly flutter, my fingertips tingle, and my heart feel light as I sensed excitement about the wheat stalks' transformation. As the machine magically cut down and then threshed the wheat stalks into two parts—the seed or grain, the edible part, and the chaff, the unusable outer skin—I experienced life, death, and transformation tangibly intertwined.

I also was an instigator of transformation. If my older cousin Mike was at the farm, sometimes we'd stand in the long grass of the ditch and catch live grasshoppers in our hands as they sprung up, then carry them between our cupped hands, still jumping, to the farm cats, who'd eagerly grab them between their paws and tear into their bodies, gobbling them down hungrily—a process we watched with fascination.

In the evenings, after supper, by the light of a soft lamp and the television tuned to *Family Feud*, I'd sit on Grandpa's lap and clean his nails, watching for signs that I was hurting him, especially when attending to the third nail of his left hand, which he had smashed working on farm equipment.

"Did it hurt?" I had once asked.

"Yeah, it hurt," he replied.

"Will it ever go back to normal?" I wondered.

"Nah, it'll probably always be like this," he answered, shrugging.

"Did you have to go to the hospital?" I asked.

"Nah, I ain't got time for that. A guy's gotta get back to work, you know," he said.

His handed-down mindset of endurance and discipline translated into many admonishments over the years: "Quit your whinin'," "Just get it done," "Enough screwin' around." For my grandparents, daily life left little time for relaxation. For them, Mother Nature was not a kindly figure but one at whose mercy they remained. Just enough rain at just the right time could signal a prosperous year ahead—food on the table, money to supply seed for the next year's crops, perhaps even enough to purchase some much-needed machinery. But too much rain or hail could wipe out their crops and their hopes, leaving them with nothing in their hands and even less in the bank. Their forbearance and headstrong determination worked as the fertilizer allowing them to plant and produce crops year after year, no matter how many fingers might be smashed along the way.

❧

One late summer day on the farm, when I was seven, I headed out back where Grandpa had transformed a tractor tire, which had rolled over countless acreage over the years, into a tire swing that was a source of joy for my cousins and me—not a bad retirement for a tractor tire. I slipped off my pink jelly shoes and tossed them onto the lawn. They rolled to a stop at the feet of a brand-new riding lawnmower, cooling down after a hot afternoon spent trimming the grass around the barn, the silos, and the dusty white farmhouse. I gripped the two cool metal chains and wiggled my hips to the tire's front edge, its warmth seeping through my sundress to my summer-kissed skin. My feet stretched down to the dirt, my muscles flexing as I walked backward until the tire stood nearly upright. Finally, I kicked out, dust flying. I folded my knees and tucked my legs underneath the tire as it swayed back, then pulled again and leaned back, blotting out the sun with my bare feet. The world blurred; the wind whispered in my ears; the sun warmed my skin; and I felt a natural connection with the source of my life and power. I defied gravity for a blissful moment at the height of my swing, until my hips plopped satisfyingly back onto the tire. Just before it was time for supper—Grandma's special buns with roast beef, mashed potatoes, sweet corn I'd shucked, and tomatoes I'd plucked—I leapt from an upswing and landed on the earth in a crouch, my whole body tingling with pleasure.

On the stroll back to the house, I kept an eye out for the wild farm cats. Without some food to entice them, most would not let me touch them. But I always tried because once in a while I was rewarded with an unguarded cat purring contentedly against my own unguarded heart—not yet broken by disap-

pointment or betrayal. That day somehow my heart guided me
to a scrawny black cat lying in a shady place at the edge of the
sidewalk leading to the house. While my grandparents would
sometimes feed the cats leftovers from supper, they never let
them get dependent on free food or allowed them in the house.
The hardy cats who survived the North Dakota winter—a
Herculean feat for a five-pound animal—would reproduce in
the spring, while those who succumbed, my grandpa would bury
in the spring. I tiptoed closer, hoping the cat wouldn't jump
and run. It didn't.

I bent down to pet the cat. It did not respond to my touch.
Cool and stiff, its entire body rotated on the pavement when
I kneaded my fingers into its hip. I suddenly realized that the
cat was dead. I snatched my hand back, having never before
touched anything dead other than a bug. I stood still, observing yet another transformation.

"Did you touch that cat?" asked my uncle in a warning
voice, suddenly appearing out of nowhere.

Startled, I stared up at the imposing, jean-clad man with
downturned lines on his whiskered face, sweaty brow, and
grease-stained knuckles. My uncle was much like my grand-
father—hardworking and salt of the earth. He was often kind
to me, recorded in pictures of him and me making snow cones
together on a child's machine. It is understandable to me now,
as a protective mother, how finding his niece seemingly playing with a dead cat would provoke ire, but at the time I simply
sensed danger and potential admonishment.

"No, I didn't," I lied. I remember this as my first conscious untruth, and I remember the way it felt—the way a lie *still* feels—in my body. My face flushed, my throat clenched, and I held back tears.

"Are you sure?" he asked again, his eyes narrowing in suspicion.

"Why can't I touch the cat?" "Will I get sick?" "What happens to the cat now?" were questions I had but intuitively knew better than to ask. Unwilling to waste more time, such a precious commodity in farm country, he said, "Well, just forget about it and go wash up for supper."

"Okay," I whispered and plodded up the concrete steps leading to the house. My head felt heavy. There was a painful hollowness in my heart. I shuffled into the kitchen, where the food was steaming on the table, but I was not hungry.

For most adults, a brief exchange like this would be inconsequential. But for me as a child the incident, which combined a first exposure to death, a confusing encounter with an authority figure, and a first lie, triggered an awakening. This was not a rub-your-eyes-greet-the-sunshine-coffee-is-ready awakening or the kind of awakening I have since learned about in my spiritual studies, one marked by bliss and enlightenment, because rather than helping me enjoy the sensory aspects of life or recall my innate connectedness to all things, it introduced me to the harsh realities of the adult world—an awakening marked by forgetting.

I forgot about my inborn connection with the natural world. I forgot about my awe of transformations, both instigated and inevitable. I forgot about my freedom and the simple joy of being myself. And, with all that forgetting, I woke up to the real world. Things and people of the world snapped into their proper places like schoolchildren coming off the playground and returning to their desks. Everything became organized into categories of right or wrong, good or bad, friend or enemy, mine or not mine. What had previously been called "experience" and "lessons" became judged, counted, and measured. I now understood that there were rules to learn, lines to color inside of, and correct behaviors to adopt.

Soon after this "awakening" I stopped picking dandelions for my mom on the way home from school because I knew they were not flowers but only weeds. I saw my parents not as superheroes who could fix or answer anything but as ordinary, fragile people who experienced sickness, injury, and failures, and didn't know everything. I became acutely aware of how much my mom spent on groceries each week, and I stopped asking for costly sugary treats. Standing in ditches catching live grasshoppers in my hands I now saw as gross, and jelly shoes as no longer cool.

I mark this day in my life as the day I forgot the essence of who I was—someone free, whole, adventurous, curious, and filled with an immeasurable love for the world around me. I also mark it as the first day of my journey to remember these aspects of myself.

## CHAPTER 5
### *Travel Scrapbook*

NOW THAT OUR HEAVIER DISCUSSION REGARDING the River of Forgetting is behind us, Rasa and I stroll back out to the precipice to witness the transformative process of creation, various majestic life-forms—planets, stars, comets—forming, existing for a while, and then dissolving back into the cosmos.

As we watch the magic unfold, Rasa reminds me, "Human beings often believe that Source—which some call the sacred, God, or the Divine—has an ultimate finale still to come. But in truth it is the ongoing cycle of creation and destruction through which its greatness is expressed in each moment."

Then I pick up where we left off in our conversation about the child ego, asking, "So what happens after my ego and I lose our connection to each other?"

Rasa collects her thoughts and then says somberly, "Once Earth Realm becomes the only valid reality for the ego, your power to influence her will diminish, and the remainder of her childhood will likely be shaped by family and societal norms.

Then you must contend with the volatile adolescent ego. Many souls lie in wait through much of adolescence, while societal forces—parents, teachers, coaches, and other authority figures—shape the adolescent ego's mind and heart."

"And then the adult ego takes over," I add, feeling slightly overwhelmed at the recollection.

"Yes, and the overconfident adult ego is a significant obstacle to reestablishing connection. Plus attitudes and forces prevalent in the time of your next incarnation, such as narcissism and the pursuit of materialism, will further obstruct attempts at communication between ego and soul."

I suddenly feel dizzy. I raise my hand to my head, where memories swarm like bees, threatening to sting. I see myself, in various human skins, never able to voice my intentions in the Earth Realm due to my ego's fear of communication with me. "Rasa, I am recalling whole lifetimes of never getting through to my ego, making me feel sadness, loss, and pain," I say.

She steadies me by briefly touching my forehead and replies, "You have had those lives, but note that they taught you lessons as well. And remember you have also experienced lifetimes filled with creativity and more successful communication with your ego." She taps my heart three times, and I feel a jolt, then I see thousands of lifetimes—each lasting but a blink of a soul's eye and encompassing adventure, creativity, wonder, and joy, fueled by dialogue between my ego and me. But whether reviewing joyful or painful lives, it soon becomes too much for me to take in so many moments simultaneously, and I realize this is one of the reasons human beings live in linear time—so they only have to focus on experiences sequentially.

Rasa takes my shaking hands inside her steady ones, and fortunately the memories cease. Then she pulls a thick book from her tote bag and suggests, "Let's revisit your memories a little more slowly, shall we?"

"What is this?" I ask.

"It is your travel scrapbook, of course. I updated the cover. It seemed more ..." she pauses, searching for the correct phrase, then adds, "positively portentous."

Last time, I remember now, a willow tree, representing a journey marked by increasing openness of mind, graced the cover. This time there is a stuffed, smiling bear with a pink heart stitched onto its protruding belly, matching one of the stuffed bears on my suitcase. These bears must be a theme of my upcoming life, I conclude.

"Go ahead, take your time browsing through the scrapbook," she encourages. "Revisit some of your past trips more leisurely than when you lived them hurriedly in Earth Realm time. Pay homage to people with whom you have interacted along the way. Trace your evolutionary path through time and space. This way you can remember more about why you have signed up for this trip."

"I signed up?" I ask, not remembering this step.

Rasa brushes her hands in the air, back and forth, as if painting a poignant scene, then replies, "As your last life faded away, your body returned to dust, and while transforming back into light and energy, you made your wishes known. The cosmos responded to your desire and carried you directly here to the precipice. But there is no Soul Realm court that will force you to honor that decision as if it were an Earth Realm contract. Human life remains what it has been for all eternity: a choice."

Reassured of my own power to choose, I spot an oak tree that has grown tall enough for me to rest against, sit down, stretch out my legs, open my travel scrapbook, and slip inside the womb of time to remember. Just placing my hand on its cover is enough to awaken memories of a great variety of past travels, journeys showing me that I've known famine and riches, power and humility, servitude and rule. I've worn the garb of landowner, farmer, housewife, and battle warrior. Out of curiosity, I've slipped into the smooth skin of a snake, the rough skin of a bat, the thick skin of a bear. Sometimes I've chosen to remain skinless in the Earth Realm, as a raindrop to be embraced by a great ocean, or slid my roots deep inside the ground to stand as a powerful redwood tree. I've bloomed as a bright yellow dandelion then transformed into its white seeds, lifted free by the passing wind. Once I chose to live as only a speck of dust, and what lessons I learned as I was swept from place to place! At still other times, to experience more of my disembodied state, I have traveled throughout the cosmos as only consciousness, free of any body or world. I have cannonballed out of supernovas, drunk rich wine from the Big Dipper, and hitchhiked on fiery comets. Some of these trips I have even undertaken simultaneously, splitting myself into factions.

But the embodied human condition holds incredible potential for reaching higher states of consciousness and attaining greater range of knowledge, both of which bring souls nearer to Source. It is this higher purpose that urges all souls to continue their often tumultuous journeys incarnated in human skin, as reflected in the lives depicted in my travel scrapbook.

As I open it, pictures spread out in panels call me to the life stories they portray. To revive a particular past life, all I have to do is touch a picture, and it feels as if I am there and events are happening now. Of course, from the perspective of the Soul Realm everything is happening now.

The first page depicts me as a bosomy elderly woman, rocking on my front porch with my beloved by my side, inviting those who walk by to come in. Having lived a bountiful life, I spend my remaining days sipping coffee while drinking in my guests' stories of struggle and triumph, longing and loss, love and heartbreak.

The next page shows images of me as a ponytailed ambitious explorer hiking up snow-capped mountains. Weariness and loneliness are reflected in my face. But from the perspective offered by the Soul Realm I can also feel the explorer's exhilaration and growing power.

On the next page are snapshots of me as a tall, pale young man dressed as a Viking warrior. Here I am a trained fighter who has outwardly shed all innocence, but self-doubt shows in my eyes. A thin, semitranslucent, bluish-gray snake, dressed up in a black-and-white pinstriped suit and blue tie, hovers just above my shoulder. Cold slithers up my spine upon recognizing the snake as Fear. What soul could forget Fear, the oldest, most cunning, most battle-worn, and least naïve of all human emotions? He is a consummate imposter; even in this picture, with his chin held high to impersonate Courage, his darting eyes betray his true nature.

I continue going through my travel scrapbook, revisiting past lives and coming across many other emotions—in snake form—that I will surely encounter again in the Earth Realm. I reacquaint myself with Guilt's sharp barbs, with Anxiety's anguish, with Shame's power to diminish, with Depression's darkness.

Rasa, watching closely, reassures me, "Their hiss is worse than their bite. If one respects their potential power, they can actually be made into allies instead of adversaries in life."

"It is clear to me that I have not always treated my emotions with respect or appreciated their purpose. Especially Depression," I say, indicating a thin skeleton of a snake draped in a dark cape. I observe that pictures featuring this emotion won't spring to life no matter how hard I press.

"Yes, given the despair it evokes it is difficult to respect Depression's purpose," she agrees, wincing at the memory of her own encounters with this emotion.

I continue flipping through the pages of my travel scrapbook, seeing many lives lived merely on the surface, all dressed up and smiling on the outside but with emotions unacknowledged and disrespected. With a flash of insight, I exclaim, "The stuffed bears on my suitcase and on my travel scrapbook—

the theme of my next life—must represent my emotions and how they've often been stuffed inside me so no one could witness them!"

"Yes, a life where emotions play an important role lies before you. Though whether you deny them or express them is left to you and your ego," Rasa explains.

Seeing my emotions from the perspective of the Soul Realm awakens my respect for them. "In the next life, I will encourage my ego to respect my emotions and even advocate for them," I promise. At this idea, my belly flutters and my fingers tingle.

"Advocating for the emotions would be a boon in the Earth Realm," Rasa replies. "Because there, as you recall, while some emotions are celebrated most are ignored or even vilified. Sure, Joy is welcome nearly anywhere—except at a funeral, of course. But try bringing Anger into a classroom or Fear into a competition!" She bends over with laughter, and I join in, conjuring up images of such breaches of Earth Realm protocol.

At the mention of Joy, I quickly search through the pictures of my travel scrapbook to find her. I soon discover that regardless of the story Joy is never too far away. Red-cheeked, bright-eyed, and outfitted in layers and shades of pink, Joy can be found even in life's toughest situations. "Will Joy be joining me in this next life, Rasa?" I ask, hopefully.

Rasa sighs, shakes her head, and says, "That is yet unknown. Every life is different. But each of your emotions will visit us here at the precipice, likely in the order of their first major appearance in your human life. You can ask them whatever questions you may have for them upon their arrival. I believe Fear has the pleasure of arriving first." She gestures toward my scrapbook.

The next time I find Fear in the pictures, he holds a small suitcase in his tail and is waving to me almost cordially. I sigh, knowing there is likely no talking him out of coming along since Fear is an essential component of human life. So I lovingly straighten his black fedora and continue on, page by page, life by life, to the end of my scrapbook. On the last page, I find a giant oak tree bursting with thick branches and bright yellow leaves, at the top of which hang four colorful lights. "Who are these souls?" I ask, pointing at the lights.

"They are the birth family I've chosen for your next lifetime, taking into account your past journeys, your current state of consciousness, and your desired growth opportunities." Rasa answers. "They, like you, will live the next life deepening their relationship with emotions. Though you will all approach emotions differently, this theme will bind you together as a family, if you agree to choose them."

I touch each light and see sequences of images related to our future relationships. One is of me, a petite girl about seven years old with brown ringlets, wearing a silky blue full-length dress and white sandals, holding the hand of a thin, elegant, blue-eyed blonde, my mother, wearing an identical dress but white sandals with heels. We are holding flowers and smiling an identical smile at an uncle's wedding.

Another sequence shows me a few years older with my father. We are in a school, playing a duet on a piano while my classmates circle around us. Though we both make mistakes, it doesn't matter. I am proud he is my dad.

Next I see images of my younger brothers and realize that though we will be very different we'll be connected by love and caring. Then there is a sequence showing me as a teenager, wheelbarrowing my second, redheaded brother around a carpeted floor on his hands before we both collapse in a heap laughing, exhausted from our play. Finally, there is a picture of all five family members gathered around a Christmas tree in a cozy living room, opening gifts with barely contained anticipation. As I feel the potent yet hidden emotions flowing through my future family members, a tear of gratitude rolls down my cheek. This, I know, is the right family for me.

Minutes later I emerge from the womb of time like one awakens from a sweet dream, following one last memory of a fire licking away the cold on a snowy night while the lingering taste of blackberry wine on my tongue cleanses from my palate the last shred of doubt about my upcoming journey.

## CHAPTER 6

## *Emotional Guardrails*

GROWING UP, I RARELY SAW MY MOM EXPRESS her emotions and certainly never uncontrollably. My dad, his eyes often welling with unfallen tears of pride or nostalgia, fought back his emotions as if they were lions and he had only a chair to keep them at bay. My dad might've been a successful general manager at work, but when it came to emotional management my mom was more successful.

One day when I was in my early teens I got a close-up look at her method. My mom, my brothers, and I were driving home from my grandparents' house on a summer evening, our bellies full with Grandma's stuffed pork chops, baked beans, and banana cream pie. We didn't need the tornado warnings on the radio or the sirens blaring around us to recognize that we faced danger. We only needed to peer out the windshield, through which we saw torrential rain, sky-splitting lightning, and black, menacing clouds threatening to sweep us away.

I imagined the inhabitants of nearby houses hunkered down in their basements, and I wished we were safe in our basement, too. If it had been daytime, that drive would've proffered sun-kissed fields of wheat and corn waving in the breeze under a sky spotted with puffy clouds looking like white angels, elephants, and giant birds. But that black stormy night all I could make out was a green sign on the side of the road that read "Christine City Limit." Having recently read Stephen King's *Christine*, about a possessed car bent toward death, I felt my heart begin to pound and hot tears well up in my eyes.

My mom stopped under an overpass as a haven from the pelting rain and asked us if we would rather wait out the storm there or slowly drive the last twenty-five miles home. We kids chose the latter. So we drove onward, behind a semitruck to help keep us from straying from our lane, and finally arrived home safely.

After we'd been home for some time, my dad called from work. I listened for my mom to tell him how we had almost died, to confess how scared we all had been. But she said, as brightly as usual, "Yes, everything is fine here." I swallowed my tears and absorbed the lesson: don't let anyone see your true emotions.

My mom's ability to drive straight through the storms of life threads back to at least 1962, a time before weather warnings and storm watchers, when she was twelve years old. Her parents, taking a well-deserved night off, had driven into town for a card party, while she and her older sister had been left in charge of the house and their younger siblings. It began to rain harder, then hail—not dime- or marble-size hail but hail large and strong enough to shatter two kitchen windows so water streamed inside the house.

Her parents, given the hazardous road conditions, explained over the phone that they could not drive home. My mom, frustrated by her older sister's hysterics, put everyone to work shoving pillows into the broken windows. From the barn to the sheds to the garage, that hailstorm broke over sixty windows, but it stood no chance of so much as denting my mom's defenses against her emotions.

Knowing this about her, I'm not surprised that she chose the vocation of nursing, where her ability to focus on the task at hand and not get swept up in emotion served her well for several decades. But she only worked part time so she could be there for us kids when we got home from school. She filled her free time with creative projects: crocheting, quilting, and sewing. Over the years, she made me a Christmas stocking with my name on it, a pink and white summer shawl, and a faux fur coat that I wore every winter day. She was also a part-time businesswoman, selling some of the things she made, like stuffed Care Bears—with official names like Cheer Bear, Sunshine Bear, Wish Bear, Tenderheart Bear, and Share Bear—on whose white bellies were sewn rainbows, sunshine, hearts, and flowers. While she often recruited me to join in her business projects, I never caught her in the act of making something personal for me. She must've done this only after I had gone to bed, for even demonstrations or words of love were kept quiet, revealed only at times deemed appropriate such as holidays or birthdays.

No one could've known that this capable, independent, uncomplaining woman selling happy Care Bears was quietly suffering symptoms of kidney failure, including fatigue and shortness of breath, because she wouldn't have confided in anyone. Finally, though, my mom could ignore her physical symptoms no longer. In 1996, doctors diagnosed her condition as glomerulonephritis—an inflammatory kidney disease—and said she would need a kidney transplant to save her life. Luckily, the needed kidney came quickly from an excellent match: her younger sister. To this day, my mom has the kidney, though doctors told her not to expect it to last more than ten years. If the doctors had known my mom better, they'd have realized that if she determined the kidney was going to last longer it would.

On holidays and many Sundays, I watched my dad, sometimes joined by uncles, brothers, and cousins, alternate between cheering and booing at sports games on TV and drinking cheap beer, a male bonding ritual I envied while I was relegated to drying dishes and scooping leftovers into plastic containers in the kitchen with my mom and aunts. Later I wondered if, in our culture, sports provided an opportunity to express pent-up emotions without judgment, allowing everyone to go back to work on Mondays purged.

However, I was not able to express my emotions like my

dad, shouting at the TV. And I couldn't do with my emotions what my mom did—hide them. Anytime I got in trouble, had a fight with a friend, received a bad grade, skinned a knee, or heard an unkind word on the playground I sobbed until my stomach ached.

As I grew older, a cunning emotion who had been waiting for a moment of confusion over how or if I fit in with my re-served family rapped on the door to my mind, and insisted, "I am the oldest and the wisest of all the human emotions, and I'm here to protect you."

"I can protect myself," I asserted.

In an effort to persuade me of my need for him, Fear began to reveal his observations about me, saying, "You are different from all other little girls. You have thoughts and ideas that stray too far outside the boundaries of what is safe or accept-able. You have dangerous dreams and imaginings that are best kept hidden. Your safest path is to not let it be known that you are a highly emotional person or have big dreams. Look around. Everyone else fits in. See their knowing smiles, their confident interactions, their genuine happiness? Understand this: you have no important purpose in this world. Everything that needs to be created has already been created. Everything that needs to be said has already been said. You can read about the amazing people who have said or created valuable things in textbooks, but you cannot become one. Because you are an outsider. Put your trust in me. Who was there for you when your uncle asked you about the dead cat, to tell you that you had to lie to stay safe? That was easy. I can do much more. I can show you how to change like a chameleon so you can pretend that you belong in this world. You can trust me never to reveal this truth, and I trust you to follow my example."

"Tell me what I need to do to be safe and belong," I acquiesced, gulping. "I don't want anything more than that."

Fear nodded approvingly and closed his proposal with what seemed like a logical series of statements: "Feeling too much makes you vulnerable. Vulnerability weakens you. The weak do not survive. And life is about survival. So you must do what you can to not feel too much, or at least not let anyone see you in such a weakened state."

Fear's arguments for my need of him were convincing enough that, after this appeal, I developed an inner belief fused so tightly with my identity that it took me years to realize it was separate and could ultimately be discarded: To live safely in this dangerous world as an outsider, I could never reveal to anyone how I truly felt. If I did, I would be neglected, discarded, forgotten.

## CHAPTER 7

# The Museum of Universal Truth and Cosmic Knowledge

Now that I have had ample time and space to review my travel scrapbook, my soul body feels warm, porous, and nearly human. I carefully put my scrapbook, Care Bear side up, into a corner of my suitcase. Given that I have officially begun packing, my decision to travel is final, and I am no longer so apprehensive as I am curious about my next adventures.

"Sëri, my friend," Rasa says as she pulls my hands to help me stand. "I have a place to show you where I have been researching my new project."

We walk down a cobblestone path, alongside a field in which golden stalks of wheat have already grown to the height of our knees.

"What is this new project of yours?" I ask as we walk.

"Soon I will tell you," she answers, mysteriously. "But first there is more for you to remember."

We climb up a grassy knoll, atop which sits an L-shaped,

two-story, white brick building with black molding around its many windows. "This looks like an Earth Realm library," I say, stumbling upon a memory.

She nods. "Depending on the soul, this building can also appear as a laboratory, an office, or even a sports stadium. Your vision of it seems to be traditional," she remarks, laughing, "but it is much more than a library. Allow me to present to you the Museum of Universal Truth and Cosmic Knowledge—the oldest, grandest, and most comprehensive library in the universe." She curtsies dramatically.

I can only stare in awe at the immense amount of knowledge contained within a single building. Is knowledge endless or finite? What can be known, and what cannot be known? Is all this knowledge available to humans or only to disembodied souls? I wonder.

Rasa makes a sweeping gesture toward the open door, and we walk through a brightly lit entrance into a foyer beneath a domed-glass ceiling. The foyer is shaped like a clock, and at the location of every minute is a different pathway. Every pathway is lined with walls on either side that extend to the ceiling. Each wall is lined with shelves; each shelf filled with books; and each book packed with stories, wisdom, and lessons.

I tour the museum slowly, shelf by shelf, book by book. My ability to read and digest the information I find is greatly enhanced in my soul form. I start with concrete topics such as history, architecture, sports, and math. This satisfies me, the way a main course satisfies. Then I move on to the less tangible subjects of imagination, love, poetry, and art—manifestations of the creative human heart that are the sugar to the starch and protein of my diet. I am most taken by the stories of how egos, together with their souls, relate to Source in its various names: God, the sacred, Allah, Krishna. I watch ancient yogis, shamans, native medicine people of all traditions engage in their practices. I observe people in forests, mountains, ashrams, and even bedrooms and offices meditate in silence for hours, reaching states of consciousness that mimic what all souls experience in the Soul Realm. I observe human beings travel on light alone through time and space. From dance to prayer to ritual to silence, there are seemingly endless ways in which Source can be revered and honored.

I come across a book with a soft burgundy cover that juts out a little further than the rest as if encouraging me to select it—entitled *Christianity: An Exploration of the History, Beliefs, and People of Earth Realm's Largest Religion*—and inspect its pages, ornately decorated with thin gold leaf. When I open it, a small triangular piece of colored glass falls out, with shards of orange, yellow, green, blue, indigo, and violet fanning out from its ruby red center. I hold the glass up to the light coming in through a window, and immediately colored light spills onto the floors and walls of the museum.

"Rasa, you have to see this!" I shout.

"I'll be right there," she yells from around a corner. In a blink, she is back by my side, a book of her own in her hands, the title of which she keeps hidden from my view. I know I will learn more about her new project when she is ready to tell me or, perhaps more to the point, when I am ready to hear about it.

"Look at the glass that fell out of this book. Is it not brilliant?" I say.

She glances at the book and glass and replies, "That is an Earth Realm artifact, likely from the window of a place of worship. It is stunning but is certainly an outsider's, not an insider's, item. It is yours to pack, but that will mean encountering Christianity during your human journey, always from the outside."

I gently place the glass on a windowsill as I consider this option. "It feels like it has value for me, but I am not sure how much." I return to the book, discover something else in it, and say, "I also found this emotion inside the book. I recognized him from the pictures in my scrapbook, always tagging along behind me, tripping over his endless to-do lists," as I stare at a short, boxy, beet-red snake whose body tapers and ends with a barbed hook for a tail, watching us suspiciously from the pages.

My old friend senses my worry, wraps an arm around me, and says in sympathy, "One does not easily forget Guilt."

"Still, though troubling he is not entirely bad," I reply, already feeling like the advocate for my emotions I hope to be in the next life. "He merely wants to stay safe, follow the rules, choose right over wrong, and his cautious voice could prevent some disastrous mistakes."

"Certainly, there is a role for him to play in human life," my soul friend concedes, "especially when the need arises to restore integrity. But to make critical decisions about your life I suggest that you follow the instincts you have attained over the ages and the magical knowing of the human body over the potentially manipulative words of Guilt."

"The human body is magical?" I ask, absorbing this idea as a contrast to ideas about the body being fragile. Then I remember books I have read about how the human body magically communicates its truth to anyone who pays attention, through communication devices like grunts, winks, crossed arms, long pauses, turned shoulders, and tone of voice that may or may not match the words spoken by a person.

Rasa further underscores the magical qualities of the human body, saying, "Since the human body is comprised of the same core materials as the universe—earth, water, fire, air, and ether—it is as mysterious and magical as the universe. In the body, each element corresponds to a different sense—earth for smell, water for taste, fire for sight, air for touch, and ether for sound. These senses are some of the best truth-detectors the universe has ever created, so let them guide you when confusion arises between what you sense is true and what Guilt tries to make you believe is true."

As she speaks, I feel the initial development of the human organs necessary for me to use each of these senses—a nose to smell, a tongue to taste, eyes to see, hands to touch, and, finally, ears to hear.

"And then there is the gut," Rasa adds, indicating a spot three finger widths below and two finger widths behind the navel. "This is referred to as the Dantian, the *hara*, the Svadhishthana, or the second chakra, in various Earth Realm traditions, though it matters not what you name it as long as you call upon it for the guidance you seek."

I rub my belly, and it responds to my touch the way a baby responds to its mother. This place beneath my navel is where all my inner knowing can be accessed. Knowledge is both knowable and infinite, I decide. It is all there to discover when we seek it, and yet we will never be finished seeking it. Like a soul, knowledge is a paradox: resolved but still evolving, whole but never complete.

"How does the knowledge transfer to the human body?" I ask.

Rasa explains, "Previous lives leave indelible marks—energetic imprints, or karmic residue. These impressions are what humans call intuition, inner voice, or gut instinct, and they are always with you, in whatever skin you take on. Such knowing without a direct reason can help you navigate darker times. But if Guilt gets his hook in you—and he will surely aim right for this place in your body—he will attempt to distort your intuition, or inner voice, and thus your sense of truth. He will invade the most private places in your mind. He will lecture you about original sin, remorse, blasphemy, and hell but offer deference only to one side of God, the masculine, and more deeply respect the power of the Church than the intuitive knowledge you bring with you."

Watching Guilt smack his scarlet lips and stare at me sends an icy chill through my soul body. I give him a tentative wave and close the book, considering its authority. I think about what I stand to gain, and what I might lose, in my relationship with Christianity and with Guilt if I pack the stained glass. But then I suddenly know what I need to do and explain, "I understand the challenges taking this glass could pose, but I feel I need the experience it might offer, even if it is only from an outsider's perspective."

Rasa laughs and replies, "See! You are already remembering how to tap your intuition."

## CHAPTER 8

## *Invasion of the Sanctuary of the Mind*

EVER SINCE I CAN REMEMBER, I'VE BEEN a vivid, in-color, action-packed dreamer. Give me a quiet, darkened bedroom, a solitary hermitage, or just a backseat during a long car ride and I'll drop into a world of pure imagination where roles, identities, and labels can't catch me. As a child, I had a wildly imaginative inner life in which I pondered, without judgment or fear, whatever showed up.

I could so easily shift between reality and imagination that I once did a test to determine if what was in my mind was to-tally private. In the living room, with my mom sitting on the couch next to me stitching something, my dad in the recliner sipping his evening beer, one younger brother on his stomach on the floor, the other already in bed, I thought of some for-bidden words then looked at my family to check for any reac-tions. Their unsuspecting faces told me they did not hear me and that I could continue living in the world of my imagination with no fear of censorship.

Once I was assured of this, my mind became my sanctuary. During the daytime, while other kids played with buckets and shovels in sandboxes or built snow forts, I created word games in my mind, exploring the myriad ways I could connect thoughts. One of the word games I played at night entailed beginning with the name of my great-grandmother, who had died when I was seven, and quickly thinking a series of word associations before circling back to the beginning, such as Grandma White, snow, sledding, fast, fly, birds, sing, school, hopscotch, friends, family, Grandma White. It was my own brand of hide-and-seek, with me hiding in the words while sleep tried to find me. Though I was later labeled an introvert after taking personality tests, I simply saw my mind as my favorite play space, my blank canvas on which I could express my creativity endlessly.

Not only was I content inside my mind, sometimes I used it as a rocket ship for space travel. Lying in my darkened bedroom at night, I'd slip out of my human cocoon, fly off this planet, past this solar system, and beyond. An invisible tether kept me connected to my body, but for a time I would experience a sustained freedom similar to being at the apex of a roller coaster, a few breathless moments swelling with possibility, freed of limits. Something deep inside me knew that such an experience of freedom, both enjoyable and terrifying, was truer to who I was than anything I could experience on earth in human form. At some point, the tether to my body would tug, and I would drop back inside my body, my heart pounding, wondering if I had traveled to the realm of the soul. These experiences made me wonder about the life of a soul perhaps younger than many. I wondered whether there was life after death, or even life before life. I wondered if I had chosen this life or if it was a wheel from which I could not get off. Time didn't exist in this expansive place—or, perhaps more accurately, all time existed, making the opportunities for adventure limitless. Soon, though, I shifted my attention from studying the natural world to observing the people who populated it. Thereafter, adult rules overtook the places in my mind once inhabited by childhood curiosities, and, as a result, my life became constrained by the norms and social constructs of my midwestern upbringing.

Though such experiences of being outside physical limitations made me wonder about the existence of a soul realm and if I had ever inhabited it, they did not prompt me initially to wonder about religion. Our family, official members of the local Presbyterian church, a simple two-story white building within walking distance of our house, usually attended services only on Easter and Christmas Eve. We would slide into a middle pew, shoulder to shoulder with our next-door neighbors, another family who seldom attended, as if there was something redeeming in our complicity. I would sit swinging my legs to a rhythm determined by the light dancing through the stained-glass windows. My parents would toss a few dollars into the silver collection tin we received, which always made me feel proud. Throughout the service we would stand and sit as directed, and hum or mouth the words in the bulletin per tradition. Even my dad, who would often break out in a loud, embarrassing rendition of "Happy Birthday" at the pizza place where we often celebrated birthdays, would blend his voice with everyone else's in a show of social unison. At the end of the service, we would line up to shake the hand of the pastor, whom I imagined deemed us hopeless. I would avert my eyes and glue my arms to my torso, hoping to get so small he wouldn't see through the barriers that Fear had helped me erect. If anyone could see through them to my true self, I suspected, it would be a man like him, a man God favored.

While my parents likely assumed it was their duty to provide us with the foundation of religious education at church, they did not elaborate on it at home. Only at holiday meals when our grandparents were present would we all fold hands, bow heads, and recite memorized religious passages, all sighing with relief at the amen. So for many years religion, like school, was nothing more to me than something I had to do. I assumed that God, his son, and the aloof Holy Ghost focused their attention on powerful people and grand events, not on me and my little life.

But one Sunday morning the pastor's announcement from the pulpit shook me awake. "God is always with you! God knows the deepest thoughts and fears in your mind!" he said, suddenly making me feel like the sanctuary of my mind had been invaded. Fear, fretting over my mind's unexpected monitor, placed a frantic call for help. Guilt promptly arrived at the doorstep of my mind, and Fear pushed open the door to invite Guilt in, saying, "God's watching and listening to everything! I can't keep him out. You gotta help me clean this place up!"

"You're right, Fear," Guilt said, frowning as he lumbered up and down the rows of my mind, "I'm an expert on God, and I can tell you that he expects a tidy, sin-free mind with only good, safe thoughts."

Fear ran about, picking up a few of my word games and dropping them at Guilt's feet. "Throw them out!" Guilt snapped. "Imagination leads to wondering, wondering leads to questioning, questioning leads to insolence, and," he whispered, "you've heard of hell, haven't you?" At Fear's defeated nod, he added, "Stick to the plan, Stan. That's my motto."

Together with Fear, Guilt combed through the contents of my mind, intent on finding something bad. They were successful. My mean thoughts about my brothers? They found them. My clever-but-sassy replies to my parents that I thought but never dared say? They found them, too. With each new discovery—trying out a curse word, saying shut up to my brothers, being jealous of my friend's bottomless baskets of Barbie dolls—Guilt clucked while Fear tapped my nervous system's shoulder to send warning signals: a somersaulting stomach, a quickened heart rate, a welling up of salty tears.

I suddenly wondered what else God knew. For instance, did he know about my cosmic travels? Guilt answered on behalf of God, in a tone of disapproval, "God doesn't approve of you running away from his kingdom any more than your parents would approve of you running away from home."

Greatly impacted by Guilt's warning, after this anytime I tried sneaking past God's heavenly lair to travel the cosmos my heart jolted with Fear, cringed with Guilt, and I snuck back into my bedroom like a thief returning to the scene of the crime, slipping back inside a body that reminded me of my sinful nature and which I realized I needed to tame through Fear's strict discipline and Guilt's constant vigilance.

And in church I began paying attention to every word of the sermon, now aware that eternity is a long time to be punished for not learning the rules.

"You hear that, Guilt? We have to fit through the eye of a needle! How are we ever going to do that?" Fear asked.

"Keri, be small and meek to fit through the eye of a needle," Guilt commanded.

"Like this?" I asked, as I crossed my legs like all the other women and held my elbows close to my body, practicing the posture I would adopt in future experiences of uncertainty, confusion, and fear.

"It's a good start," Guilt said, approvingly.

"I'm going to get more answers," I replied frantically. "I've been invited to go to a real church, a Catholic church. Let's all go, we'll learn more. Maybe that's where we belong."

Wondering if Catholics might know better how to obtain eternal safety than Protestants, I attended a Catholic church with a friend and her family. I entered its massive, ornate doors and gaped at the high, domed ceilings, the rich atmosphere, and the golden glow. The pictures and carvings of Jesus were familiar to me, but the myriad pictures of his mother Mary were new. All I knew about Mary was that, due to her virginity, she had been chosen to be the mother of Jesus. I slid quietly into the hard-backed pew next to my friend. I brushed my fingers across the gold-rimmed Bibles and hymnals lining the pew. Organ music piped down from the balcony that extended directly to heaven. The smiling priest floated in wearing a crisp white robe, a purple sash, and a scarf with gold tassels. This was authentic religion—the real Kraft macaroni and cheese, not some cheap imitation—I decided.

Once the service began I stood, sat, and knelt following the congregation's cues. However, I discovered that, as an outsider, I was not invited to take Communion or receive the kind words and warm greetings that accompanied it. I accepted that while truth and knowledge might exist here I was not granted access to them.

Years before at my grandparents' I had walked my bare toes far underneath me to gain enough leverage on an old tire swing to rush through the air so fast and freely that I felt as if I could reach up and touch the sun. But during my first time attending Catholic Mass I tucked my scuffed white flats underneath the pew and my stomach constricted with confusion.

"Keri, you know what to do," said Guilt.

I did. I slipped on my "can-do, don't complain" attitude and tidied up my mind. Now instead of playing mind games before bed I recited a desperate prayer: "Please, God, forgive me for all my sins. For all those things I have said and done today that I shouldn't have. Even when I knew they were wrong, I did them anyway. Please forgive me. And if there are any sins I forgot about please forgive those, too." Was I God-fearing? No, not me. I was God-petrified.

I know many people for whom the same message—God is always with you—is a comfort, not an invasion of privacy. I have friends and family who embrace the sights, sounds, smells, and messages of churches, synagogues, mosques, and other places of worship. I acknowledge that my imagination took great liberty to interpret the meaning of the Presbyterian pastor's words as something sinister and the members-only Communion of the Catholic church as a personal rejection. But none of this can change the fact that to me churches have never felt safe. Inside their doors I have always felt simultaneously exposed and claustrophobic, though despite these uneasy feelings I eventually got confirmed in a church, was married in a church, and had both my daughters baptized in a church. Perhaps this reflected my desire to belong or my general tendency to respect the authority of religion. Most likely it was a combination that had me keeping one foot in the church, hoping someday my reluctant second foot would cross the threshold into the promised land.

# PART II

## Growth and Adaptation

The skin, being pliant and flexible,
enables humans to grow as they shed old skin cells,
between thirty and forty thousand per day—
like a snake shedding old skins of childhood
and assuming new, shiny skins of adulthood,
ready to continue forging a new path in the world.

## CHAPTER 9

# *Endless Curiosity and the Great Truth*

IN THE MUSEUM OF Universal Truth and Cosmic Knowledge, I am remembering more about who I am. I recall that I am an eternal searcher for, and lover of, truth, an urge that has led me on treacherous journeys across time and space, especially to the Earth Realm, where diverse cultural traditions are said to embody truth, expressed through religions, prophecies, books, manifestos, and philosophies. In the Earth Realm, entire cultures are built on a collection of shared beliefs that people call "truths." But these cultures fade as soon as new beliefs gain power, which only proves the truths on which they are founded are anything but solid. Lifetime by lifetime, skin by skin, I have spoken for these incomplete truths, fought for them, died for them. But they were not the Great Truth—for where the Great Truth would unify, they have divided. Where the Great Truth would collaborate, they have conquered. And where the Great Truth would embrace, they have often separated, punished, and demeaned.

Over my lifetimes, it seems clearer to me that rather than clinging to these small truths, or beliefs, humans would be better served by empowering their own endless curiosity to attain new knowledge and forge new ways of being that honor the earth and all people without prejudice. Becoming curious about life and others could spur personal growth, invoke communal compassion, and even promote the ever-elusive but much-coveted peace on earth. Yet taking on established truths as my own—my unique way of piecing together the Great Truth—further clarifies why it felt right to pack the stained-glass chard ensuring my encounter with Christianity.

I say to Rasa, who has patiently waited while I savored my past, recalled my concerns, and remembered my mission, "I must resume my search for the Great Truth, which is more slippery than I had anticipated. Yet I feel it is my calling to continue the search."

Rasa, a twinkle in her eye and slight smile on her lips, replies, "Let me see if I remember. You are seeking the truest truth, the key that opens all life's doors, a truth so wise it can end all misunderstandings and crises."

"That's the one!" I exclaim joyously at hearing my own sentiments echoed back to me.

"Well then, since you have remembered this mission, it is time to call for your animal accomplice." Before I can ask questions, she whistles.

At first, I see and hear nothing but the sparks and bangs of creation throughout the universe. But then, from a distance, I hear galloping, followed by howling. I feel a tingling sense of anticipation in my body. Finally, I see a wolf in the distance, looming larger and larger, with two piercing silver eyes. I watch in awe as this wild creature leaps, her long, sinewy legs cutting through the air, stretching farther than any earthly wolf could dream. With her muscles rippling and her fur shining, she is the picture of health and energy. She lands, soft as a whisper, by my bare feet, her lips drawn back to display two rows of sharp white teeth. I stare at her, her curiosity feeding my curiosity, her wildness inciting my wildness.

"Endless Curiosity!" I exclaim as I greet my truth-seeking companion. I run my fingers through her thick coat and scratch behind her sharp, pointed ears. "How you've grown since our last trip together—what was it, two, three lifetimes ago? What an appetite for truth you must have now! Why, you look ready to cause a revolution!" Memories of our journeys together awaken in my mind. Never have I ventured on a quest for the Great Truth without this powerful companion, whose appetite for truth knows no bounds. She has kept me searching when I wished to give up, reminding me that I am fiercer, wilder, and stronger than the ever delicate human skins I embody.

Watching our reunion, Rasa glows with pleasure. Then she takes from her tote bag an instruction booklet and says, "While it is my honor to reunite you with Endless Curiosity, it is also my duty to remind you of how to care for her once in the Earth Realm. It says here that it is critical to feed her well and often. Her diet must not consist of too many empty calories—gossip magazines and the like—but contain substantive nutrients, such as philosophy, science, nature, religion, and art. Neglecting her needs for too long will cause a hunger in her, and by extension in you, that can be quite perilous. And yet feeding her the substantive stuff will prove challenging, too, since so many times and places in the Earth Realm now ban wild creatures like her. In pursuit of nourishment, she is bound to get you into some trouble now and then."

Rasa tucks the booklet away then continues nostalgically, "There was a time in the Earth Realm when she and others in her pack—Thirst for Knowledge, Dreams of the Future, Unlimited Imagination—were respected and cherished. But you are going to a time when knowledge, and the curiosity that incites pursuit of that knowledge, is under siege. Indulgences of the intellect and the imagination are downplayed in favor of building reputation and status, sometimes at any cost. Remember that power in the Earth Realm is held by only a few at the top of a hierarchical society. Known as Authority, their power—and, by extension, knowledge—is dependent on humans not challenging them by asking too many questions. You can be sure they will call your wolf rebellious and disruptive, though what they mean is intimidating. Be ready, truth seeker, because Authority will try to frighten Endless Curiosity away and often succeed."

"But she will always come back to me or I can go to her, right?" I ask.

"Always—depending on your awareness of her absence and the need for her," Rasa affirms, to my relief.

I look into my wolf's luminous eyes and ask, "But where will Endless Curiosity go when she is not by my side?"

In answer, Rasa only smiles.

"What is it?" I prod.

"Over lunch, I will tell you about my project. Until then the answer to your question is that there will be a safe place for Endless Curiosity to go in difficult times. Even if the two of you are apart for days, weeks, or perhaps years, I guarantee her well-being upon your reunion," Rasa asserts.

Feeling confident about her care, I turn to another concern. "'Endless Curiosity' is a bit of a mouthful. How about we call her..." I pause as I recollect the etymology of the word *curious* from one of the books I have read and then add the suffix for the feminine, "'Curiosa.'"

"I think that's a fitting name," Rasa says, "and much easier for a child to say, certainly."

"Do you like it, Curiosa?" I ask my wolf, who barks her assent.

"Do we have time to take another trip through this museum? There are some books Curiosa will surely devour," I say.

"We have all the time in the universe," says Rasa, smiling. And then we three saunter down yet another aisle of the Museum of Universal Truth and Cosmic Knowledge to further explore the knowledge of the universe.

## CHAPTER 10

*Hungry to Learn*

BOOKS, BY LETTING ME INTO THE MESSY, imperfect inner worlds of fictional people when I was a child, served as a direct portal to the most intimate truths of human life. Even given the often vast discrepancies between the characters' lives and my own, I could empathize with the characters in a way I rarely could with real people. In elementary school, as I browsed each monthly book order form deciding which books to choose, my belly would flutter, my fingertips would tingle, and my heart would feel light. And my mom, without exception or objection, would write a check to cover the cost.

The books—Nancy Drew and Trixie Beldon mysteries, Beverly Cleary and Judy Blume coming-of-age books, the *Little House on the Prairie* adventure series, the *Sweet Valley High* teenage romance series, and later, in high school, V. C. Andrews, Stephen King, and Anne Rice novels—were magic carpets that flew me to foreign lands and alternate worlds. They told stories of heroes and heroines overcoming fear to reveal their courage.

They showed the messy, imperfect feelings of people that more closely resembled my own interior than the polished veneer of individuals I usually saw at the grocery store or the front of a classroom. Where my dad had used sports as an outlet, a way to express his emotions, I learned how to use books as an inlet, a way to honor mine.

It was through books that I met a wolf with silvery eyes named Curiosa, who thereafter became my companion on all my searches for adventure, knowledge, and truth. Perhaps to grown-ups she was imaginary, but to me she was as real as the books themselves. She first appeared sniffing at some book I held in my hands. Though her hunger was palpable, I was comforted by her presence and unafraid. She gave me a lick and curled up by my feet, her ears turned backward toward me, listening, pondering with me. The two of us loved children's books, but we were equally fond of schoolbooks—though we had different approaches to, and attitudes about, learning. My relationship with teachers, coaches, parents, or any other authority figure was simple: I followed their rules and did my work; they gave me good grades and permission slips. Seeing authority figures as the keepers of knowledge and truth, I both respected and was intimidated by them. I knew by this time that the world was populated with two kinds of people: people who set the rules and people who followed them. It didn't seem that hard to understand and honor the hierarchy. On report cards, some teachers described me as a good student, well behaved and a joy to have in class, but other teachers barely had reason to know my name, and that's the way I liked it—remaining invisible while quietly indulging in knowledge, nearly unseen in the back of the classroom.

But Curiosa didn't bother with rules and cared not for protocol. She was willing to confront my teachers directly to get the clarity and completeness she needed to feel satisfied. Many of her nudges I could ignore, but some were too strong to resist. If a teacher's lecture was confusing, my hand would fly into the air, waving for attention I didn't want just to satisfy Curiosa's need for things to be correct. Fear, to whom such behavior seemed out of line, would panic and say, "Put your hand down this instant! Everyone is looking at you! You don't know what to say!" But once called on I—absent of Fear—would express a thoughtful question or observation that impressed even me, though perhaps not my teachers, who probably preferred me being a quiet joy, and certainly not my classmates, who preferred we go to lunch.

Curiosa's hunger in the classroom only grew as I did, and by the time I reached puberty she was unpredictable and nearly insatiable. Given the fact that I was now breaking out with acne and wore thick glasses, this was exactly the wrong time for me to be more visible. But even while I mustered the nerve to pose a question now and then, I never dared to express anger, annoyance, or a dissenting opinion. One time our teacher told us to expect a bonus question on a social studies quiz, and I spent additional time studying. When the question turned out to be "Name the teams playing in the Super Bowl this year"—a ridiculous question that had nothing to do with our social studies chapter and besides,

I didn't follow football—I suppressed my anger, fearing it would get me in trouble.

Actually, at the time it probably would've been harder for me to get into trouble than to stay out of it. Common excuses of troublemakers confused me: "I got carried away," "It was a momentary lapse of judgment," or "I wasn't thinking." How does someone stop thinking? I wondered. I wished I'd have known. I was always analyzing information, or reflecting on the last thing I had said or done, or worrying about the next thing I might say or do. My thoughts never stopped—one reason, I believed, I avoided trouble.

That is, I avoided trouble except once when I was fifteen. My best friend, Jackie, and I were out for a weekend afternoon stroll. We walked up a small hill to the new high school being built over the summer to be ready by fall. Excited about our class of 1990 being the first to attend it for all our high school years, we peeked in some of the windows, imagining which of the rooms might be our homeroom. Then Curiosa led us around to the back, where we tried the door and found it open.

For maybe the first time in my life, I didn't think and instead followed Curiosa inside the school. We ran around exploring, imagining, laughing, our faces flushed. Then a car drove by. The adult male driver and his female passenger looked up at us. We waved. A few minutes later they drove by again. We thought that was weird, so we ducked. The third time they drove by staring at us, we decided we'd better leave. Curiosa whined but followed us to the hallway that led to the door. There stood a Fargo police officer. Jackie and

I, both feeling fear and confusion, looked at each other help-lessly.

The officer growled, "What were you girls doing in there?"

"Nothing," we answered.

"How did you get in?" he asked as he studied the door.

"The door was open," we mumbled.

"Open or unlocked?" he asked, challenging us to lie.

"Unlocked," we clarified.

"This door shouldn't have been unlocked," he stated, glaring at us and pulling out his radio. "Tell me the truth, now, how did you get in?" he asked again, after putting the radio away.

"The door was unlocked," we said again.

He stared down at us and replied, "Well, you girls will have to come with me to the station."

"Jail? What have you done?" chided Fear, rushing around in my mind.

Up until this point, Jackie and I had both thought the officer, content that the encounter had sufficiently frightened us, would realize he was dealing with innocents not delinquents, and send us home. We followed him to his car and crawled inside. The door locked automatically when he shut it. We stared at the grates that separated the back seat from the front. We were no longer joys to have in class. We were criminals. The ride to the station was probably less than five minutes, but it felt much longer. Jackie and I kept glancing at each other, our faces reflecting the unspoken words: How could we have been so stupid? What are we going to do now? I glared at Curiosa, who kept looking out the window, thinking this was a pleasure drive.

I was relieved but embarrassed when my dad arrived at the station to pick us up. He talked with the officers, his salesman persona working its magic to get us out of trouble. Ultimately, we were not charged with anything. My dad didn't speak on the drive home, but once I was alone with him he lectured me on how I'd disappointed him, how he thought he'd taught me the difference between right and wrong. If the floor had opened up, I would gratefully have let myself be swallowed by it.

Fear warned, "Everything I told you about staying small and invisible you just ignored. The problem is that wild animal you've been palling around with lately. School, particularly, is no place for wolves! You can have her or you can have safety, but you can't have both."

I agreed. As a child, Curiosa had been a fun fellow adventurer, but her inquisitive nature disrupted my logical thinking, which I needed if I was going to stay safe as I grew older. Keeping her around would only lead to a life of more trouble, like a trip to the principal's office, which, for me, would've been equally as mortifying as sitting in a police station.

Consequently, when school started that fall and Curiosa tagged behind me as usual, I led her to a tree just outside the school building and said, "Listen, I'm sorry, but you have to wait out here." She looked up at me, head cocked to the side, confusion clouding the silver gleam of her eyes. I leaned close and whispered in her ear, "I know, but you're not allowed in school anymore. You'll get me into more trouble. You ask too many questions, you disrupt my thinking, and you make me too visible. Just wait out here, and we can read a book tonight at home, okay? Besides, I'm growing up now, and I need to start fitting in. You don't see any of these other kids bringing wild animals to school, do you?" She stretched her long legs out to lie down on the pavement, lowered her head, and exhaled heavily.

Fear applauded my decision, saying, "Without Curiosa, you will be free from asking anything but the most basic questions in school, free to stop seeking clarification or correcting misstatements, Keri. Without her, you will be free!"

Fear was right to a certain extent—I felt some freedom in not asking questions. But a more important sort of freedom was lost in that early exchange of Curiosa for my safety. Despite her penchant for getting us into trouble, Curiosa represented my curiosity, my freedom to explore both seen and unseen aspects of the world. Without her, the world was no longer a place to explore but instead a confusing, potentially threatening place, which, like the dead cat from years before, was not for me to touch.

Nevertheless, there were occasions during the rest of my school years when I was still able to go on adventures to other times and places through my book portal. Senior year my English teacher introduced me to many classics, including *The Scarlet Letter, The Divine Comedy, Death of a Salesman, To Kill a Mockingbird, Lord of the Flies*, and *Animal Farm*. In this class, we students slipped into the various skins of the characters we read about. We often empathized; we sometimes criticized; we always hypothesized. We discussed why the world was struc-tured the way it was, and suggested that perhaps we, brazen and bold, would be the ones to change it into a more equitable, caring place. And I, the shy introvert, the back-row girl, began to consider taking a front-row seat, my soul shining through my eyes. Though I still looked to others to toss logs on my fire for this kind of shapeshifting, I already had an inkling that one day I would build those fires by and for myself.

## CHAPTER 11

### *Defining Ambition*

AFTER WE FILL OURSELVES ON KNOWLEDGE, the three of us—Rasa, Endless Curiosity, and I—stroll back to the precipice. The landscape has changed substantially in our absence. The River of Forgetting still rushes below, and the flowery settee remains with my open suitcase on top, so I place the piece of stained glass from the Museum of Universal Truth and Cosmic Knowledge inside. But the field of wheat has disappeared, and in its place a carpet of grass has grown in a uniform bright green color, no higher than two inches, each blade immobile despite the gentle breeze, stretching down wide fairways and around small streams. Two parallel rows of colorful flags delineate a route through the grass.

"What we have here seems to be a hint of one of your chosen paths," Rasa says, laughing with delight, as if even she did not expect this transformation. "It looks to be quite an ambitious path indeed! Sëri, why not give it a try?"

I note that I am standing behind a bright yellow strip painted on the grass, with the word *start*. Somewhere in my consciousness I hear someone shout, "Ready, set, go!" In my feeling state alone, I run from the starting line until anticipation changes to exhilaration, followed by a sense of power and the sounds of crowds cheering. But suddenly fatigue sets in, then desperation mixed with sadness and an undertone of anger, and at the finish line, only relief and exhaustion. Breathing heavily, I reflect on these emotional states. "Rasa, you called this an 'ambitious' path. But ambition should lead to feelings of power and accomplishment, should it not?"

"Well, that would depend on your definition of ambition. Perhaps you could locate some books that provide definitions to ponder," she suggests.

I quickly conjure up three sources from the Earth Realm, where the word *ambition* originated. "Here we are," I say victoriously. "First, the definition in the *Oxford English Dictionary* is "A strong desire to do or achieve something." According to *Merriam-Webster's Collegiate Dictionary*, it is "An ardent desire for rank, fame, or power." And Dictionary.com—a digital dictionary—calls ambition "An earnest desire for some type of achievement or distinction, as power, honor, fame, or wealth, and the willingness to strive for its attainment."

I flick my wrist to make the books disappear and catch Rasa grinning. "Okay, I'll play this game," she says, conjuring up a book of her own from the ether entitled *Consolations: The Solace, Nourishment, and Underlying Meaning of Everyday Words* by David Whyte. She opens the book and reads, "Ambition is frozen desire; the current of a vocational life immobilized and over-concretized to set, unforgiving goals."

This definition more closely matches the feeling state of my race than the ones I have found. With a sense of foreboding coming over me, I ask, "Is it possible to skip over this ambitious path and try slower, gentler, more inclusive paths instead?"

My friend winks and replies, "You are becoming more and more human every moment, focusing on the difficulties but missing the gifts! Of course, you can make any changes you wish since this is your life. But no one can outrun the lessons you must learn—whether or not you actually run, they will catch up to you."

Taking a different view, I say, "I read a few books about running while we were in the museum. Other people truly enjoy running. They even speak about their pursuit of a runner's high. Their energy seems to come from a more genuine place."

She nods and replies, "You are speaking of the difference between ambition and passion. Two humans could be doing the same activity, but for one it is a passion while for the other it springs from ambition. The person acting from passion will find energy a bottomless resource, sourced from the soul. The person acting from ambition, however, will find they must continually feed their fire with self-discipline, sourced from the ego."

I cringe, imagining the many harsh forms an ego's discipline is likely to take. We sit together for a moment as I attempt to make peace with this information. Then she brightens and says, "I have an idea. Let us review a couple scenes from your next life before you conclude that this runner's path has no value for you."

"That would be a great help," I reply. "But how do we—"

Before I can ask how it is possible to watch a scene that has yet to happen, Rasa waves her hand, and suddenly there appears before us an old leather bus seat. I laugh at how out of place it seems in the beauty of the Soul Realm. "Where did you get that old thing from?" I ask.

"Trust me, it's more comfortable than it looks," she replies, grinning as we cozy up together on the worn seat. An engine roars to life, and the seat begins to bounce and sway gently. She waves her hand again, and a screen appears, making it clear there is much more for me to remember about the magical possibilities of the Soul Realm.

On the screen, a scene unfolds of a large yellow school bus rolling down an interstate highway through sparsely populated towns. Fields of wheat, corn, and beans fly past the windows in a blur. Only an occasional green exit sign points the way to a fast-food restaurant, gas station, or rest stop. Inside the bus are about twenty-five children dressed in various layers of green clothing, as well as three coaches and a scruffy driver wearing a baseball cap, who appears grateful that all the noisy teenagers are sitting in the back. They are playing music on what I hear the children call ghetto blasters. I find the girl who is me, a petite brunette with blue eyes and a ponytail, about sixteen in Earth Realm years. She is hunkered down in a leather bus seat, like I am now, sharing snacks, stories, and jokes with the people around her.

Once the screen fades to black, I remark, "It's comforting to know that I will have an abundance of friendships on my ambitious path. Thank you for showing me this."

"Oh, there is more! And even these are simply two scenes of hundreds available to choose from," replies Rasa.

A new scene flickers onto the screen. There, legs outstretched in the middle of a game field, are four girls dressed in brown, blue, black, and white, and a girl who is me, wearing green. The four will be competitors in a few moments, as indicated by the papers they hold in their hands, but now they commiserate about sibling squabbles, prom dress shopping, and homework. I notice something expand in my soul body as, immersed in this moment, I unexpectedly feel oneness and connection on a path defined by fierce ambition. As the scene fades, the feeling of oneness remains.

"The power of the human experience never fails to surprise me," I say, placing a hand over my heart.

Rasa looks at me, her eyes, like mine, full of tears, and replies, "You will forget this once your journey is underway. But this knowledge will be available to you again when you look past the curtains of right and wrong, beyond 'should I have' or 'shouldn't I have.' Remember this: When humans seek differences and competition, they will certainly find them; but when they seek unity and cooperation these occasions are in plentiful supply, too."

Still feeling the warmth of friendship and unity, I say, "It does seem that this ambitious path offers some truly soulful gifts."

"Indeed," she agrees, as we both stand up and the bus seat vaporizes.

## CHAPTER 12

# *Following the Course of Ambition*

By high school, I had settled into a vanilla kind of life. I was a nice, quiet, obedient girl, but one who would likely not be remembered for anything. I got awards for being a book return champ, though not for much else. However, I was safe, not a threat to anyone, and I did not incite anyone to threaten me. Ironically, this unflavored existence stirred up my emotions rather than settling them.

"She's boring, Fear," Guilt grumbled. "If she's going to take up space on this earth, she ought to at least try to make something of herself. Anyone can get good grades. And reading books will take her nowhere. She needs to *do* something! Fear, our girl needs some ambition!"

Fear replied, "But she is an outsider, Guilt. Being seen is risky for girls like her. People could criticize her, be suspicious of her motives, or, worst of all, see her in her wholeness—her light and dark, her faults and strengths, all her emotional truths. Guilt, people could even catch glimpses of her soul, despite the protections we've put up!"

"Being unseen is risky, too, Fear. Think about it," Guilt drawled.

Fear thought about this, envisioning what it would be like for me if my life stayed vanilla, then replied, "You may be right. What if she can't stand out in the real world, where there is not enough love, security, or opportunity to go around? But ambition is also dangerous!"

"Are you kidding?" Guilt answered, sneering. "It's getting exposed as an outsider that's dangerous! Listen, an ambitious path, one approved by authority figures—running!—could cover up the fact that she's an outsider."

"Well, she does have her mother's endurance, as well as her father's drive and commitment, to draw from," Fear acknowledged as he drummed his fingers on his chin, and Guilt knew he'd succeeded.

As children, we trust and love unconditionally. But by the time our parents, society, and Fear and Guilt implant their voices within us we believe the world is a barter system that functions by the principle of scarcity. Ambition, we are told, is the key to surviving in a finite and conditional world. I, like most girls, received this additional warning: Be sure to stand out but fit in; be inspiring without making others uncomfortable; push boundaries but remain within the rules of society. The inference was that once girls became too ambitious they were a potential danger to those around them, too assertive, disruptive, annoying—crazy bitches in the making.

Consequently, choosing an ambitious path was clearly risky but one Fear deemed less risky than the possibility of being left behind. So Fear handed me a plastic water bottle and said, "Drink up, my girl."

"What is this?" I asked, looking at the bottle.

"That's ambition," he replied.

I drank the liquid and, wearing a runner's jersey borrowed from the school locker room, stumbled into the blinding, blaring, dog-eat-dog arena of competition. In this arena, even second place was considered a loss, and no one dared to quit no matter what. Praise was heaped on those who pushed through pain, overcame obstacles, and disregarded weakness. In no time, I was jostling elbows with the best runners in North Dakota. I was no longer acting like an outsider but instead doing something worthy of attention and approval, which arrived in the form of ribbons, medals, my picture in the paper, and my name read over the school intercom.

Like many runners, I was soon addicted to running, not to the activity per se but to the hamster wheel of ambition, praise, validation, belonging, needing, competing, and around again, an addiction complete with cravings, seasonal withdrawals, and a one-pointed attention on nothing but the next fix.

I was on fire—soon in more ways than one as a red rash of hives spread all over my body. My doctor told me that embarrassment would not kill me and neither would the hives, that since I was neither feverish nor having trouble breathing there was no reason to quit running. But the hives were ugly, so I tried to hide them beneath my warm-up clothes until the very last second. For each race, we'd take off at the sound of the gun in a tornado of arms and legs amid shouts and cheers. I'd slide into my signature springy stride, my ponytail bouncing rhythmically against my back. I'd go through my mental checklist: drop my shoulders, let my arms swing loosely, clench and shake out my hands.

"No pain, no gain. Quitters never win, and winners never quit!" Fear would say, egging me on by repeating quotes from the cat posters hung up in my bedroom.

I never thought about quitting, even in races where I "hit the wall" and experienced sheer agony, when my brain disassociated from my body, when I felt trapped in quicksand like a slow-motion horror film, when my mom's face on the sidelines told me that I looked exactly how I felt. I'd still force myself to stumble over the finish line and collapse into my coach's arms, thinking, "Wait'll Dad hears how I did today; he will be so proud of the reputation I'm building for myself."

I began describing myself as the driven runner others told me I was. Never mind shin splints, pulled muscles, side aches, blisters—or hives. Never mind the truth that I acknowledged only in the quiet, lonely stretches of the races: that I didn't enjoy running nearly as much as I let on. But by this time I no longer remembered that ambition was something I initially nurtured to combat my feelings of unworthiness. Now I told myself I was a naturally competitive person. When someone described me as ambitious, it filled me with pride and made me wonder if I could achieve even more. So I pushed on and on.

Soon, though, my running life led to new, unexpected problems. One of my teammates didn't like me because she'd been running longer and I had beat her on my first race. Another schoolmate didn't like me because she was friends with that teammate, and told me I was a show-off.

Guilt clucked his tongue and said, "Keri, you are not supposed to be showing off. Humility is a virtue."

Fear added, "Before you may not have been seen, but you were not disliked either. Now that you've put yourself out there you've created enemies! Perhaps you should go back to being invisible."

"Fear, it is too late for that. I have a reputation to uphold," I answered.

Today, having long ago set aside my running shoes, I have no regrets about my role as a competitive runner. Through running, I learned about teamwork, training, and the intimate connection between the mind and body; I made many friends and challenged my limits. But it's equally important for me to acknowledge that this role taught me to believe that my body had no value other than the doors it opened for me, that my body was a currency to trade in my pursuit of whatever abstract thing—acceptance, accolades, love—I wanted most at the time. I projected onto my body the insignificance my ego feared. As my ambition inflamed the deeper tissues of my body and mind, I became less concerned with uncovering my desires and dreams and more motivated by paths that rewarded me with tokens of self-esteem no matter how short-lived. I became less excited about a moment for what it was and more focused on measuring the moment's potential to raise myself up in society. Instead of a free-wheeling wild child who followed her heart and curiosity, I became a woman who cared too much about what others thought of me—just as likely to hold back love for others as to give it, as likely to judge them as to befriend them. Much later I was able to see that, though in general our society views ambition as a valuable and résumé-worthy attribute, too much emphasis is placed on ambition's intended goals of success and increased status rather than on the potential costs of attaining these things. Ultimately, I envisaged it this way: if our ambition and the actions that stem from it inflame our bodies and separate us from others and our true selves, then it is a poison not a nutrient.

## CHAPTER 13

### *Robe of Authority*

"Schand schill now, or wil never ged dis done!" Rasa says, holding a row of sewing pins in her mouth while pinning the fabric draped over my body.

"But Curiosa isn't having any fun!" I argue playfully on behalf of my wolf, who is hidden somewhere beneath the piles of fabric scattered about the precipice.

"Jush one more minude," my soul friend requests, placing a final pin. "Now, isn't this the most gorgeous robe you've ever seen?" I stare at my reflection in a full-length oval mirror. We have been so engaged in dialogue and adventure I had not realized how much more human I now look. I bring my hands to my face and rub them along my cheekbones and chin, down over my throat and shoulders, feeling the soft, supple skin forming over the bones. I comb my fingers through my chestnut hair then run my hands over my fully formed breasts and hips, enjoying the emerging curves of my feminine shape. The robe, which opens and closes with a zipper up the front, is made of satin and silk in shades of yellow—lemon drop yellow, gold crown yellow, champagne yellow, and wheat field yellow. It covers me from shoulder to toe and then some, being nearly three inches too long.

"Rasa," I say carefully. "It's beautiful, but I'm afraid it's too big."

"Why, what makes you think that?" she asks in an amused tone that worries me. I indicate the extra fabric hanging past my hands and feet, expecting her to shorten the robe.

Instead, she seems pleased with it as is. "I assure you that it is just right. Once you are in the Earth Realm, you will seek out mentors who can help you grow into your robe of authority."

I slip the robe off, hand it to her, and observe, "Oh, so that's what Authority's role will be in my upcoming life? Usually Authority just tells me what to do."

Rasa laughs, her hand slapping her knee, accompanied by thunder sounding and lightning flashing in the sky. Rasa's laughter is clearly one of the universe's favorite storms, one in which all the celestial bodies love to participate. I, too, take this moment to enjoy the light show she creates through her pleasure.

"Oh my, your candid admissions are one reason I love you so much," she says, as she finally wipes her eyes dry with a pink handkerchief. "But you are making a common mistake of conflating Authority with mentors, when there is quite a distinction. A good mentor will have your best interest in mind and will help you expand your personal authority, challenge your perception of boundaries and limits, question your most deeply rooted beliefs—the ones Fear and Guilt implant at a young age—and encourage you in your quest for truth."

"And Authority?" I ask, even as I begin to fill in the pieces of this storyline.

"Authority is comprised of people tasked with keeping the status quo—whatever that might be. They dislike change and prefer to silence dissenters rather than listen to them. Authority's job is not to help you grow but to operate the levers of power from which Authority benefits. Perhaps," she muses, "with the insider knowledge they gain, these same souls will one day tear down the systems they now build up."

"Oh, can you imagine a whole planet full of souls ready to tear down power structures and hierarchies?" I ask, my eyes sparkling as Curiosa howls at the possibility of such a revolutionary development.

"That day is surely coming," Rasa replies, with a knowing wink.

My soul body responds with a thrill of adventure, but then I return to the issue at hand. "Will it be clear which souls are mentors for me and which ones are the more worrisome authority figures?" I ask.

"That's a good question for which there is no simple answer," she replies. "These roles change shape as the circumstances change. A good friend can play the mentor for a while, as can an authority figure. On the other hand, sometimes a human being wears the skin of a mentor but is actually working on behalf of Authority. The only way to discern is to ask yourself this question: Are they trying to keep me from my own robe of authority, or are they helping me grow into it?

Even this question is not so easily answered, as intentions are complicated by ego. This intention-sniffing task can perhaps best be delegated to your hungry companion here." She nods in the wolf's direction. "And delegation is all the rage in the Earth Realm these days, from what I gather. There is nothing Curiosa would love chewing on more than the intentions of Authority!" Rasa gives another thunderous laugh.

"Curiosa doesn't respect Authority?" I ask. "Has she been harmed by authority figures?"

"Yes, and so have you, if you recall," Rasa answers. "But it's not truly a matter of disrespect. Rather, Curiosa respects anything and anyone who lets her be herself and treats her kindly. The problem is that her nature is not tame but wild. Like any Earth Realm animal born in the wild, she is not beholden to the authoritative structures set up by humans."

Rasa smiles at me and adds, "When you and your ego have grown enough together to wear this robe of authority, just call for it. It will then fit you perfectly, I guarantee." She folds the robe and tucks it inside her tote bag.

CHAPTER 14

## *Putting Skin in the Game*

UNLIKE MANY OF MY CLASSMATES, who were sad to leave the familiar routines of high school or nervous about their future, I was thrilled about the prospect of change. I had always wanted to live my life as if it were a Choose Your Own Adventure book, an interactive format that invited readers to participate in the story by making choices for the protagonist and thereby determining the outcome. As a child reading these books, I had felt empowered to choose my own adventure. But, having spent thirteen years in the same school system, I'd built up a reputation and grown some roots whether I liked it or not.

During this transitional time, I didn't have mentors to advise me on how to expand my options. My running coaches knew me only as an ambitious runner, and encouraged me to keep running. While my dad was supportive, his advice was colored with phrases that sounded like Guilt—"earning worthiness," "building up a reputation," and "proving myself in the world." At a Career Fair when I was a senior, I had felt drawn to vocations in psychology and philosophy, probably because these paths reminded me of the feeling states I'd had as a child when I'd left my body and traveled the cosmos; but I understood these disciplines were not viable career paths for me as they were too emotional, uncertain, and undervalued. So by the time I graduated from high school I had settled for adventures with predetermined beginnings and endings, having chosen a college just across the river from Fargo, where I joined the cross-country and track teams.

It's possible I might have seen that storyline through to the end, had it not been for a soul-stirring lunchtime conversation with a friend during my sophomore year. After hearing my thoughts about classes for the upcoming fall semester, she let me in on a secret, which, I could see by the rebellious shine in her eyes, she'd been dying to tell me. "I won't be here next fall," she confessed.

"Why not?" I asked, wondering if there was some problem in her family or with her boyfriend, though such explanations seemed unlikely.

Glowing with enthusiasm, she leaned in and explained, "I'm transferring to the University of Minnesota next fall. I got into the business school there."

"Tell me more," I replied, surprised at such an odd decision.

"Well, for one thing it's a more prestigious school, which means better opportunities after college. But also I think living in The Cities will be fun—there'll be new places, new people, a whole new beginning!"

At the mention of new beginnings, I felt my belly flutter, my fingers tingle, my heart lighten—feelings I knew by then indicated affirmation. I asked, "Will you live on campus?"

"I don't know yet. I was thinking of getting an apartment."

"Do you need a roommate?" I asked, grinning at Curiosa, who was suddenly by my side.

Granted, the world boasts far larger cities than the Twin Cities of Minneapolis and St. Paul. But to someone who had lived their whole life in Fargo, The Cities might as well have been London or Paris. I thought finally I'd be able to transform into anything I wanted, out from under the watchful eye of Fargo folks.

"Four-lane highways! Drugs! Gangs! Crime!" a familiar-sounding voice insisted.

"And who might you be?" I inquired.

"I'm named Logic," the voice stated.

Another vaguely familiar voice chimed in, "You'll have to start over, meaning college will take five years instead of four; you'd be throwing good money out the door."

"And your name is?" I asked.

"They call me Reason," he huffed.

"I see right through you two. You are not Logic and Reason but Fear and Guilt. You have two choices: come along and try not to bother me so much or stay behind," I chided.

"It's not too late to remain in a secure place!" Fear suggested, challenging my desire for adventures.

"If you move away, you will hurt your mother's feelings," said Guilt, trying to make me feel selfish.

I sighed and replied, "Guilt, please don't make this about whether or not I love my parents. My mom will be excited for me, and my dad would've loved an opportunity like this. Pack up—or better yet, don't bring any of the past with you. We'll start over," I said.

"Well, what should we do about these things?" Fear asked, holding up my runner's clothes.

"I'm done with running, so we won't be wearing those anymore," I answered decisively.

As Fear and Guilt, so accustomed to leading the way, slunk away, Curiosa growled happily, her pupils wild with possibility. While she rolled on the floor with pleasure, I felt empowered. I was finally going to choose my own adventure, not for a fictional character in a book but for my own life.

A few months later, with my credits transferred and my car packed door to door, we drove to The Cities. I cranked up the radio. Curiosa stuck her huge head out the back window, lapping up fresh air. Neither of us looked in my rearview mirror as the small town in which I'd been born and raised shrunk away to nothing. And I didn't hear a peep from Fear or Guilt during the entire drive. I likely assumed that I'd vanquished these childish emotions for good, but I now know that they were busy making plans for their future, just like I was.

❧

After another graduation, this time from the Carlson School of Management at the University of Minnesota, I was no longer running but was prepared to "kick butt" as a businesswoman in the corporate world. It didn't much matter who I worked for as long as there were opportunities for advancement.

One afternoon I saw a posting for an internship, and a woman named Kathy told me briefly over the phone about the kind of work available, something about insurance, CEOs, and deferred compensation. I didn't understand what she was talking about—I'd never studied these topics in my finance classes—but I trusted that it would all make sense once we sat down for an interview.

"So does this sound like something you'd be interested in?" Kathy asked.

"Yes," I replied. "I'd be happy to come in for an interview."

"Well, this sort of *is* the interview," she said, laughing.

This role change was almost too easy. Like Clark Kent entering a phone booth and emerging as Superman, I slipped out of the temporary but necessary skin of college student who wore jeans and T-shirts to the role of businesswoman who wore pantsuits with matching pumps, purchased using a shiny new credit card.

My company designed deferred compensation plans for highly paid executives of large companies, who always "maxed out" their annual allowable pre-tax 401k savings plans, leaving them few other good options for pre-tax savings. The plans, which allowed these men to defer percentages of their salaries or bonuses in exchange for either variable or fixed interest, depending on the plan, were funded with Corporate Owned Life Insurance (COLI). Each executive who opted into such a plan had to undergo a thorough physical exam and apply for life insurance owned by the corporation, which was the beneficiary of the policy. This arrangement was a win-win-win-win for the executive, the corporation, the insurance company, and us through proceeds received for fees and commissions paid to my company's principal partners. There was so much winning, in fact, that eventually the IRS tightened the tax laws.

The creative people at the top designed the plans, while as an intern, and eventually a full-time administrator, I was responsible for organizing, analyzing, and tracking the data for clients; making reports; and calculating payouts upon death or retirement. But the systems we used to track data, which required regular manual checks, were not nearly as creative or flexible as the people who had designed the plans.

When I finally understood the kind of company for which I worked, I explained my job by saying, "I help rich people get richer." It wasn't exactly what I would've chosen, but it was a job that paid $25,000 a year, and I told myself nothing else mattered as long as it put me on the path to fulfilling the American Dream. Besides, my working environment was enviable.

The headquarters for the company was in Los Angeles, while our branch in Minneapolis only had eight to ten employees, so we were less like co-workers and more like a family. Because I was the youngest and newest, everyone became a mentor to me. I had a man who could help me understand confusing interest calculations, a man who showed me how to write more efficient Excel formulas, a woman who could help me fine-tune my client communication skills, and Kathy, a hands-off supervisor who was willing to explain for the hundredth time the difference between whole and variable life insurance policies. The patriarch of our family, Steve, was a charming man in his mid-forties who reminded me of a dressed-up, trimmed-down mountain man. He seemed to see right through me from the start—reading unasked questions on my face, gauging my confidence by my body language, knowing when I understood something and calling me on it when I was only pretending. Being seen this way was humbling and a little intimidating. "Hi, Keri," he'd bellow playfully whenever I tried tiptoeing past his office for no other reason than not wanting him to bellow, "Hi, Keri." Depending on his mood, which was fluid and affected all of us the same way the gravitational pull of the moon affects the ocean, he'd either go out of his way to make me more comfortable or point out my discomfort, making my face burn. Because Kathy was between us, I didn't have to go to him often, but whenever I did, even though it was hard, I always walked away a little wiser.

Steve set the tone of our office, and it was one of work hard, play hard. It would be pin-drop silent all day, and then suddenly at 4:30 p.m. he would send a joke through email, and we'd hear laughter from his office. Soon it would be like a club party, everyone replying to the email, and then we'd all convene at one person's desk to socialize before going home for the day.

Once I saw Steve on a big stage in Los Angeles, where he seemed to reach superstar stature. He was unintimidated by the powerful men higher up the hierarchy, his presentation style was relaxed, and he didn't fill empty space with ums or uhs. He was a role model for anyone interested in public speaking, and was savvy about more general things, too—like packing. One time when I traveled with him by air to meet with a client, he waited with me for my luggage at the baggage claim, using the time to offer me tips on how to pack a carry-on next time. He was the mentor I'd always dreamed of.

Under his tutelage, I was empowered and given space to grow. Life, I thought back then, was no more complicated than a simple barter system: I needed to put some skin in the game, and, in return, I would be rewarded. I had indeed chosen my own adventure. I just didn't know it would soon include an introduction to corporate ladders. Had I known, I'd probably still have anted up. What is life about if not taking some gambles along the way? Many things about me have changed over the years, but one attitude has remained unchanged— deal me in.

## CHAPTER 15

### *The Story of Shame*

Rasa opens her tote bag and digs around inside. After taking out chalices, recipe cards, tissues, divining tools, and a few bottles of wine, she pulls out a fat book with gold lettering on the binder and explains, "Another emotion is ready to greet you, my dear. He is in this storybook I checked out from the Museum of Universal Truth and Cosmic Knowledge entitled *Astonishing Soul Stories through the Eons: An Anthology.*" Flipping through the pages, she adds, "This book contains inspiring stories of overcoming obstacles, starting anew, and seeking support, including a story about the trials of a young woman who, after traveling a long way from home, is flattened beneath the influence of Shame for a while, seemingly unable to escape his weight, but she takes a chance and . . ." She stops to look at me, my head tilted. "Well, I'll let you read at your own pace," she says, handing me the book.

"Oh, this is my story," I acknowledge, noting goose bumps rising along my arm. I shake my head with a mixture of awe and dread at the picture of Shame, a whalelike snake gazing at me through hooded eyes from the page. "Shame is something of a legend in the Earth Realm, is he not?" I ask.

"A legend, to be sure," Rasa says, nodding. "He is the ancient master who causes the mighty to fall under the weight of their egos. He has long taken pleasure in exposing an emperor's underlying nakedness. He roams the underbelly of society, getting involved with anything from petty gossip to dangerous crime and corruption. He revels in highlighting human weaknesses, after which he can dissuade people from further acts involving creativity or curiosity." She lowers her voice and adds, "He's adventure-averse, you see."

"How does he differ from Guilt?" I ask.

"There definitely is some connection between Shame and Guilt," she answers. "They both, for instance, have an acute sense of right and wrong. But much of Guilt's work is private and internal, resulting in small corrections and a deepening sense of integrity. He invokes feelings of remorse, which usually prompt humans to make amends. Though it may not always seem like it, he has an eye toward personal improvement. Once his energy is properly understood, he can be put to good use."

"And Shame?" I ask, as he blinks his cloudy gray eyes at me.

"Shame is often imposed from the outside, as others become witnesses to our wrong actions. And Shame goes further than simply judging actions as wrong and then seeking improvement like Guilt. He judges the whole person as good or bad, worthy or unworthy. As a result, Shame can trigger disappearing acts that last for days, years, or even lifetimes."

"Guilt is a reminder, a tap on the shoulder, while Shame is a face-first shove into the mud," I mumble.

"Indeed. And yet, Sëri, Shame also needs an advocate for his role in human life. Try to understand his messages without letting him stop you from living your life. Ultimately, though it may sound paradoxical, Shame can help develop your inner moral compass and self-respect."

"But how is that possible since he clearly seeks to break those things down?" I question.

"When anything is broken down, it leaves room for something stronger to be built in its place. And to be without Shame is not any soul's goal," explains Rasa, shivering at the thought.

I scan the story, seeking an approach to Shame that could work for me in the coming Earth Realm life.

Rasa advises, "Although that story has unhappy moments, remember that there are ways to heal the wounds caused by life's struggles. And that is what we must discuss next." She then pops open a bottle of the pinkest rosé I have ever seen, pours some into a large white tulip, hands it to me, shrugs, and adds, "This could take a while."

## CHAPTER 16

### *Planting Strength*

ONE DAY STEVE ASKED US ALL TO COME to the conference room for a meeting. Because of his foul demeanor of late, the mood around the oval table, the site of our usually jovial lunch discussions, was heavy with dread. He shared the news that the company planned to centralize its administrative functions at the home office in Los Angeles and that those of us in administration had the option to relocate or leave the job. At the mention of a possible new adventure in California, my belly fluttered and my fingers tingled, an unmistakable affirmation from my body.

The fact that our work family was being broken up was sad, but I also felt a sense of relief. I had left Fargo for Minneapolis hoping for broader pathways, but my path had instead narrowed since I'd taken this job. Plus, the longer I stayed, the greater my risk of exposing weaknesses I had kept so diligently hidden—the constant and exhausting work of a perfectionist guaranteed to one day fall apart. The more I settled into a routine, the harder it would be to keep up the façade of a businesswoman passionate about helping rich people get richer. I thought that as long as I kept zigging and zagging, no one could truly know me and I couldn't really hurt or disappoint anyone. This job transfer, I figured, was just the right zig at just the right time.

❧

Though my body was still stuck in a cubby in downtown Minneapolis, my mind and heart were already on the beaches of California. But before we transferred I received a new client for whom I had to do summary reports. The year before, this job had been done by a coworker, and the reports were fine. But driven by Curiosa and perhaps friendly competition I thought I could fine-tune the system, paying no attention to the adage "If it ain't broke, don't fix it." I set out to enhance and automate the system. Under stress due to deadlines yet sure that I had tested the new system well enough, I imported the data and mailed the reports, without asking anyone to review them first.

When my client called the next afternoon to tell me that one of her executives had said his statement was incorrect, upon investigation I discovered that many of the statements were, in fact, incorrect.

"How could this have happened? What a disaster!" Fear roared.

My stomach began to turn, my heart pounded, and I began to sweat in an office where the thermostat was set at sixty-eight degrees. Like a runner gunning for that final home stretch, I felt the familiar shift of my adrenals into high gear. Now, though, there was nowhere to run. This panicked, paralyzed feeling was not new to me—I'd experienced it in classroom settings when Curiosa brought me unwanted attention. But back then, not only would I have had no tools to address anxiety, I didn't even know what to call it.

That afternoon I remained glued to my chair considering my very limited options. I couldn't sweep the mistake under the corporate carpet. I couldn't tell the client to toss the statements and let me begin again; it would take time to more fully investigate what had gone wrong and redo them, and I had new projects with their own due dates. At 5:00 p.m., no closer to an answer, I went home to my apartment.

Sitting cross-legged on my bed next to a much-subdued Curiosa, I called my dad for advice. After I explained what had happened, he suggested that I not wait until the next day to tell Steve but call him at home. He said I'd sleep better knowing I'd have some help. I hung up and forced myself to dial Steve's home number.

"Hello?" Steve answered.

"Steve, it's Keri."

"Hi, Keri. What's up?" he replied.

His warm voice made it all the harder to reveal the truth. I imagined him munching on popcorn with his gorgeous girlfriend by his side as they watched *Seinfeld* and could almost see him sit up straighter and click off the TV as I told him the story.

With a hint of hope in his voice, he said, "Just tell me

the CEO's and president's statements are correct. Tell me you checked and double-checked those."

I would've given anything to tell him that at least one of those was correct but had to admit, "No, I didn't check them indiv—"

"Dammit!" he shouted.

Dreadful silent seconds ticked by. I covered the mouthpiece to muffle my sobs.

Then Steve said in a monotone voice, "Figure out what happened. I don't care how late you have to work. Then come to my office and explain how something like this could've happened. And you can kick yourself all the way to California."

I interpreted this comment to mean he was angry but too busy to punish me himself so he was delegating that task to me, which, of course, I was more than capable of. I also interpreted it to mean I wasn't fired, probably because it was too difficult to do now that the paperwork for my transfer to Los Angeles had already been submitted.

After we hung up, I stopped trying to hold back the sobs, which came in painful waves.

"Get rid of that dangerous animal. I've been saying so for years," insisted Guilt.

"But she's my companion, my friend. Without her, who will I become?" I argued, defending Curiosa. "Do you just want me to become some automaton who can't think creatively? So I made one mistake—!"

"This was not just any mistake, Keri," Fear corrected me. "This was a Great Mistake."

"There was no need to reinvent the wheel," Guilt added. "Creativity only leads to trouble."

I looked at my wolf, snuggled up on my bed with so much untapped adventure yet in her bones. Feeling my gaze on her, she curled her lips up into an innocent smile. But I now acknowledged the risk of keeping her around. Fear and Guilt were right: the corporate world—like schools and churches—was no place for a wild creature like Curiosa.

"C'mon, Curiosa, let's go outside," I said, reluctantly.

She stretched and jumped off the bed, excited about where we might be going this time of night. I walked her outside, where Guilt had conveniently set up a kennel. She looked at the kennel and then back at me. Her head down, her steps slow and painful, Curiosa walked into the kennel. I locked it and walked away.

"Good job, young lady. Doesn't that feel better?" asked Guilt when I returned without my childhood companion.

"No," I answered honestly.

"Well, that's called retribution. I bet your client doesn't feel too good, either," said Guilt.

My dad was wrong. Whatever sleep I got that night was fitful. I was anxious about the call I'd have to make to the client the next day and the moment I would have to tell Steve what I'd begun to realize: there was no mistake in the system and no one to blame but myself.

The next morning, a new emotion arrived. "Why are you here?" Guilt asked. "I took care of the problem already by locking up Curiosa."

Shame oozed through my body, making me feel like vomiting. "I don't want you here," I said, looking at my swollen eyes in the mirror. "You're too oppressive."

"You don't have to like me, dear. But you'll grow used to me," insisted Shame, saliva dripping from his mouth as he spoke. Then he said in a syrupy voice, "I see the problem. Your arrogance level is far too high. And your risk-taking level is off the charts! You want too much; you're reaching too high, thinking you are the star of one of your childish adventure books! But you're just a scared little girl. I'm going to have to give you a very poor job review indeed."

"I know I made a mistake, but I only wanted to try something new," I sputtered.

"If you don't silence yourself," he interrupted, "I will expose you further so everyone will see the naked truth: You are nothing but a fraud. You have wasted everybody's time and betrayed their trust."

Shame succeeded in lowering my self-esteem significantly during those last weeks before my relocation. I stopped eating lunch with my work family, who did not reach out to me in a conciliatory way. I feared I'd been revealed as the outsider Fear always told me I was. When I finally flew to California, I obeyed Steve's command and kicked myself throughout the flight. The lesson I took from this experience proved my childhood motto from Fear correct and likely imprinted it more deeply in my psyche: without constant and careful monitoring of my behavior, thoughts, and emotions, I would be neglected, discarded, and forgotten.

But now that I am in the stage of life that Steve was then I see that he could've used my Great Mistake as an opportunity not to shame me but to teach me. He could've talked to me about how easy it is to make mistakes when we're rushed, and how we need to ask for a second set of eyes to review our decisions even when we feel confident in our work. I was a new employee, while he had had years of experience. So while I did fail him, looking back I see that he failed me, too.

This experience triggered a dark, lonely period of shame, which temporarily stunted my growth and discouraged me from undertaking anything innovative. However, I also learned the valuable lesson that underneath their important titles authority figures and mentors are regular human beings, susceptible to the same forces of anger or fear that all of us are, and realized that when the answers, approval, permission, and validation we seek do not exist in any other individuals in the world, we begin looking inward, seeking a higher personal authority. Thus the incident was a powerfully transformative one, like taking a combine to a wheat field: it looked as though everything I'd worked for was gone in an instant, but it gave me clean, rich soil in which I could start over, and this time plant some inner strength.

# PART III

## Wound Healing and Regrowth

*When the skin is broken,*
*the entire body becomes involved in healing.*
*Blood rushes to the area and clots,*
*eventually forming a scab that defends against germs.*
*Wounds must be thoroughly cleansed*
*if healing is to occur;*
*otherwise, they can cause an infection far worse*
*than the original wound.*

## CHAPTER 17

### *Hemostasis*

DURING THE SUMMER IN CALIFORNIA, I began a workplace romance. Colleagues at work arranged for Todd and me to meet during a lunch hour. They squeezed the two of us in the middle of a round booth until our bodies touched then watched eagerly to see if we'd hit it off, and we did. After this we began flirting via the work email. He challenged me to a road race, so I laced up my running shoes one more time. I challenged him to play pool with me, conveniently forgetting to tell him I had grown up with a pool table in the basement. One evening, while out with a group, we ditched them, grabbed a six pack of beer, climbed on top of the roof of my rental house, and gazed up at the starry sky. As evening gave way to the cover of night, we admitted that our jobs, lives, and futures looked nothing like how we'd pictured them in college when we had been confident and enthusiastic and that we feared our dreams had been unrealistic or we'd been naïve. Such mutual honesty changed our bond from a cautious courtship to a committed relationship within weeks.

For my twenty-fourth birthday, Todd booked a surprise gondola ride for us in Newport Beach. When I saw the boat floating peacefully by the dock, messy emotions that I'd dammed up for months rose and overflowed, taking my date-only mascara with them.

"Are you all right?" Todd asked.

I wasn't sure how to answer that question. I knew he'd been planning my birthday celebration for several weeks, barely able to contain his excitement. Still, I had not expected Italian singing, water lapping up against a boat, and a basket packed with wine, cheese, and crackers.

It wasn't that no man had ever done anything kind for me before. In high school I'd had two boyfriends. One had bought me red ceramic roses because, as he said, they would never die, like his love for me. Corny, maybe, but as a seventeen-year-old I found it touching. The other had regularly brushed and braided my long hair and waited at home until I returned from cross-country practice. While I had cared for both of them, I had not loved them the way they had loved me, so I had ended both relationships.

After moving from North Dakota to Minnesota, I had shed my reputation as a stuck-up bookworm and introverted Goody-Two-Shoes with high grades, whose middle-class parents had never divorced or abused her so what right had she to complain, and reinvented myself as a flirtatious, extroverted college student who didn't need to limit herself to only nice guys anymore. I traded a dating life filled with flirty phone calls, beers shared in the bed of my boyfriend's pickup, and ice cream sundaes on school nights for public outings with guys I'd met in online chat rooms, dating multiple men at the same time, and the bar scene where loud music pounded away my insecurities. Flirting with strangers who had no preconceived notions about me let me become whomever I wanted—and I wanted to be wanted. After so many years of trying to be invisible, it felt good to be seen; and after so many years of playing by the rules, it felt good to break them.

What I had most likely needed when I moved away from home were intimate, female connections. But breaking into established women's friendship circles was nearly impossible; making friends with men was easier, faster, less complicated. So I told myself that I preferred male company to female company. I'd been lonely, but had someone suggested I was lonely I would've scoffed and told them that what they called lonely I called self-reliant. Still, I wished I'd had someone—a mentor, a teacher, an older friend—to suggest that my disregard for my body was perhaps something to explore.

With the men I dated, I did receive the human connection I longed for. But by the ends of evenings expectations always surfaced. I could feel the shift in a single look, a hand on my knee, a brush against the side of my breast. I believed that I was making my own choices, empowered in my sexuality, and that my sex life, though a little behind schedule, was "normal"—a term whose definition I now question.

When my first boyfriend, a professed Christian, had asked

me at age sixteen to have sex, I had said no, God wouldn't approve, and inquired if he wasn't worried about that, too? He had laughed and said he did worry but then broke up with me. This had seemed normal.

The boyfriend who had braided my hair had accepted the answer that I was waiting until marriage to have sex. But our bodies were on fire for each other. Instead of intercourse, we had bent the definition of sex to our mutual satisfaction. This had also seemed normal.

By the time I had changed my mind about having sex, at age twenty, it wasn't because I'd finally found the right guy but because I'd grown tired of waiting for marriage, which seemed decades away. I decided I'd just pray for forgiveness after any sexual encounters. I knew intuitively that the guy I had chosen to sleep with wasn't going to stick around, nor did I hope he would, but the sex had been consensual. I had cried a little but had told him he didn't have to worry about that, and he hadn't given it another thought. We had both assumed it was normal when afterward I drove home alone, first having to scrape the ice off my windshield after he had fallen asleep.

Following my move from Minnesota to California, my habits hadn't suddenly changed, so neither had the results. One man I had met in a bookstore, a devout Christian, had told me that if we were to become a couple he would be the "coach" and I would be the "player" in our God-approved relationship. Though we'd be loved equally by God, he explained, he expected to be the sole decision-maker, while my grand purpose was to be a supporter. I have to admit, given the stress I'd been under and the heavy pressure of Shame after my Great Mistake, his offer almost appealed to me—but not quite.

Then Todd entered my world, and my dating life, which had been in a very dark winter, skipped over spring and bloomed into summer. When I first met him, I saw only a good-looking, clean-cut, preppy fraternity guy. I'd long avoided men like this—for a reason. The ones I had known were shallow, drank too much, and rarely acted independently of their friends. When I learned Todd actually had belonged to a fraternity in college, my hopes sank. But in the months we dated I shared many more truths and vulnerabilities with Todd than I had with anyone in years. I'd heard tender stories from him about the topics that mattered to me most—life, death, love, and loss. I was no longer role-playing, so I didn't feel coerced to flirt or engage physically in any way that did not come naturally to me. He saw into me—in that same intimate way my Minneapolis boss, Steve, had, but instead of racking my nerves it calmed them.

So when Todd surprised me on my birthday with the gondola ride I stood on the dock wondering how to explain my rush of emotion to someone else when I could barely grasp it myself. The fact that he believed me worthy of consideration and tenderness after seeing the real me reminded me that I had at one time believed myself worthy—if not of tenderness, at least of consideration. In answer to his question I settled for, "No one has done anything like this for me in a long time."

"You deserve it," he said. He took my elbow and guided me into the boat, and back to my sense of self-worth.

My improved sense of self-worth soon led to the realization that I had never really wanted to help rich people get richer. Mindful that it was wise to secure a new job before quitting a current one, I began to interview, making up appointments to excuse myself from work. Within a couple weeks, I received a generous offer from a company in Newport Beach, California. Between the work and the pay, this job would likely have given me another shot at achieving the American Dream. But I hesitated, asking for the weekend to consider the offer.

Meanwhile, a friend of Todd's who had recently moved from California to Portland, Oregon, invited us for a weekend visit. Our two days there, with our surroundings so green, clean, cozy, and quaint, seemed light years away from the ubiquitous Spanish-tiled roofs and endless sprawl of Los Angeles. Feeling fancy free at what would soon become our favorite brewery, the two of us pondered what it would be like to start over in Portland, agreeing that life should be about adventure, wonder, and passion. I felt my belly flutter, my fingers tingle, and my heart lighten.

Though moving to Portland before securing a new job seemed risky from the perspective of the businesswoman in me, a part of me that I couldn't yet name knew it felt more right than risking my sanity and self-worth working for a company I didn't care about or taking a new job in a state that had never felt like a home.

Todd, who had never lived outside California, was also excited to try something new. So we plotted our escape from corporate hell and dreamed of choosing our own adventure.

We wondered what we, just two crazy kids in love with each other and with life, could make possible with only hope and trust as currency. Thinking that perhaps our youthful dreams of a life of passion and adventure hadn't been so unrealistic after all, we assured each other that we could deal with mundane details like jobs after arriving in Portland.

"Hurry, go back and take the new job before someone else gets it! Such a leap of faith is too risky," warned Fear.

But in that moment I felt familiar breath near my leg. "Curiosa! You've come back! I'm so glad you found me!" I shouted, hugging my wolf then rubbing my nose against hers and scratching behind her ears. She thumped her tail and panted with joy. Curiosa devoured the crazy ideas I slyly fed her under the table, while Todd and I clinked our beer glasses toasting to the thrill of adventure. When we left, the three of us let our hair, or fur, blow in the breeze as we rode in a rented convertible to sign a lease on an apartment just outside Portland.

"What are you doing? You're not even engaged, let alone married! I liked the guy who said he'd make the decisions for you," Fear chided.

"Who do you think—" Shame tried.

"I get to choose my own adventure, my life—not you," I asserted, more confidently than usual.

Back in my Los Angeles basement cubby the following Monday morning, I called the hiring manager from the Newport Beach Company and said, "I want to thank you for your time, but I'm going to pass on the job."

"Are you sure?" she asked, sounding surprised. "Because we can negotiate the pay and the start date."

"Thank you, but I'm going to move out of state," I said.

"Do you have another job offer?" she inquired.

"No, not yet, but I'm sure it'll work out," I insisted.

And I was sure it would work out. I was still young at twenty-four. I had a partner I trusted. Plus I had a college degree, a midwestern work ethic, a howling wolf to lead me on this new adventure, and a perfectly good pair of bootstraps.

## CHAPTER 18

### *Anger's Gift of Illumination*

IT IS NOW LATE MORNING, a quiet, meditative time in the Soul Realm. The River of Forgetting's roar has settled into a rush. Birds, their bellies bulging with seeds and nuts, snooze along the precipice's edge. My soul friend and I, too, have been resting beneath the leafy trees. But suddenly Rasa taps my shoulder and says, "Sëri, you must see this. I think your ego may be in trouble." A red plastic cameralike object is pressed up against her face. The words "3D Viewfinder" are printed between the two lenses. Inserted into the top of the object is a disk with dozens of images embedded in film around its edge, and as she presses a black lever on the side the disk rotates the images.

She hands the object to me. Carefully bringing it up to my eyes, I see myself as a young adult sitting in a boardroom. I find my ego beautiful. Her caramel hair, all one length, touches her shoulders and is parted down the middle, with the sides swept away from her blue eyes and held in place with clips. She wears a taupe suit that fits her nicely and a pair of low-heeled shoes. Her nails are unpainted, and her face is lightly made up with blush, eyeliner, and mascara. She looks like a young businesswoman, if a bit out of her comfort zone.

"What am I looking for?" I ask, since this scene seems ordinary as far as Earth Realm experiences go.

"Keep clicking. You'll see," advises Rasa.

As I click, the images move forward and back in time. "Wait—how is this happening since I have not yet jumped into the River of Forgetting?" I ask.

My soul mate laughs and remarks, "Well, you both have and haven't. Remember that linear time was invented in the Earth Realm, whereas the Soul Realm is disentangled from such constructs, making it possible for us to access any space and time we choose."

"That makes sense," I answer, chuckling, "though explaining that to a human might be like a butterfly explaining its access to a third dimension to an ant!" I return my attention to the images, clicking until I find what Rasa apparently wanted me to see, a scene in which my ego's face reflects confusion mixed with sadness, disappointment, and fear. Around the table are men and women at least ten years older, whose intentions toward my ego do not seem good. On the table in front of my ego sits a stapled agreement, which I read.

"Why, she cannot sign that," I say. "Signing something means that you agree with it, and she does not agree with that. They cannot force her to sign, can they?"

Rasa shakes her head and explains, "She does not know, at this point, what they can and cannot make her do. She is so accustomed to obeying Authority that although something doesn't seem quite right she's considering taking Fear's advice to just sign and avoid any more trouble."

"I see Curiosa is in the room with her. Surely she will help my ego understand that this situation demands a strong no," I say.

"Curiosa is perplexed more by everyone's facial expressions than by the details of the meeting itself," asserts Rasa.

"What about the robe of authority? Has she grown into it yet?" I ask.

"No, but if she can speak up for herself here it would certainly further that growth," explains Rasa.

"I will send her a message for no," I say decisively.

Rasa replies somberly, "Body heat would not be powerful or quick enough. Nor do you and she yet have a relationship in which you can communicate with more complexity. But you can still help her. I have an idea that may be risky but could work."

"Life is nothing without taking some risks. What do you have in mind?" I ask.

Rasa explains, "On your behalf, you could send in Anger. He is, after all, the emotion most interested in justice. With your guiding influence and his natural abilities, he can help her awaken her instincts. Then she will see the truth and have the power to say no."

I think about it. Anger, like all the emotions, has a clear purpose in human life. Situations like this one, where good intentions, goodwill, or even a good heart cannot triumph, are where he shines brightest. "Yes, please call Anger to me," I request.

"Certainly," Rasa says, and whistles loudly. Instantly, within our formerly calm space the wind picks up, the trees rustle, and all the small birds fly away. Then Anger, the dragon emotion, the most feared and ruthless of all emotions, cuts diagonally across the sky, riding tendrils of his own blinding rage.

We wave and holler to calm him down, but nothing works. I stare directly into his flaming eyes. Feeling eyes upon him, Anger shakes his head from side to side and squirms in midair. He lasers in on me, unafraid and loving. He tilts his head, and a look of cautious recognition spreads over his face. I extend my arms to him and open my palms. First, he breathes fire in an attempt to frighten me away. Then, when that doesn't work, he teeters between curiosity and avoidance. After a while, his claws retreat, the color of his skin softens from blistering red to blush rose, and he tumbles through the air like a kite set loose, finally curling up at my bare feet. I pet his scaly, scorched skin. Then I kneel down next to him and whisper in his ear. "I need you to deliver a message to my ego in the Earth Realm. Go easy—try not to frighten her. Simply motivate her to look more deeply behind facades and the roles everyone is playing. This is what I want you to say . . ."

After I finish, Anger lifts his eyes to mine. Emitting puffs of smoke from his nostrils, he says gruffly, "I'll do it, Serene."

"Thank you, Anger," I say, and tuck the Viewfinder disk, labeled with the correct Earth Realm date and time, securely beneath one of his scales.

As we watch Anger fly off toward the Earth Realm, I wonder about the danger of the fire power he carries, and I ask Rasa about this.

She replies, "Left to his own devices he is hazardous, most surely. But when taken seriously and not dismissed too readily Anger can inspire organization, collaboration, and connection, all of which are needed to create change and awakenings in the Earth Realm. Look closely, Sëri, and you will discover that Anger has often been the initial spark of energy behind great works of art, music, and healing. Anger's fire is what lies behind many great human acts of courage, creativity, and curiosity. And one day, when you have fully understood and integrated him you will be able to employ his passion to generate compassion for yourself and others. Then you will fully realize his power and let him illuminate darkness."

"The fire itself is a neutral power and not a danger to those who carry it. How it is channeled and directed is what humans must be mindful about," I conclude.

"As an advocate for Anger, Sëri, I see how this explanation alone could help reduce some of the stigmas from which he suffers," Rasa assures me.

## CHAPTER 19

### *Inflammation*

ONE WEEK INTO MY FOUR WEEKS' NOTICE to leave my job, my supervisor, Jane, popped her head into my cubby and said, "Follow me, please." I felt like I was in trouble but didn't know why. Since my move to California, Shame had assured that I'd kept about as low a profile in the workplace as possible without actually disappearing. Curiosa followed behind as we wound our way up a spiral staircase to the second floor then into a windowless conference room, where several men and women, all in suits, stared up from their papers, not smiling. Had I made another Great Mistake? I wondered. I gulped and slipped into a high-backed leather chair close to the door, with Curiosa beside me. My fingernails were unpainted, and I felt Shame redden my face as I compared them to those of the women around the table with their fresh, bright polish.

Curiosa sniffed at a stapled two-page document before us, then Jane said, "Keri, there are a few things we need done before you leave. And we'd like you to sign this agreement."

I scanned the faces around the table for clues about what was happening, but except for Jane's seemingly forced smile all offered only neutral facades that revealed nothing.

I read the document and saw that at the bottom of the first page was a typed pledge stating that before leaving I would complete the projects on which I had been working. Was this reasonable? Did they not understand that whether or not I signed papers I would always finish my work? I wondered. Then I turned to the second page and saw a pledge that I would reimburse the company for the moving expenses it had incurred on my behalf. How could they make me agree to that when they never even gave me the job they'd promised me? I thought. As part of my transfer agreement, I had been guaranteed a data analyst position in which I would be working more with the back end of the business and less with client relations yet I was still just an administrator.

Someone handed me a heavy-duty roller pen.

"Do what they say!" squealed Fear.

A disembodied voice said, "Sign, please."

At that moment, a powerful emotion awoke inside me. Until then I had lived small, trying not to cause trouble. I had been strictly adhering to the trade agreement between the world's authority figures and me: I obey their rules and expectations, and they provide positive feedback and safety. Yes, I was quitting, yet I had given four weeks' notice to ensure a smooth transition. But as my superiors were pressuring me for no apparent reason, I suddenly deemed my agreement with authority figures null and void. Fuck them, I thought.

"Hey, young lady! Watch your language!" berated every voice inside me, from my parents to my teachers and coaches—and even God.

But then Anger hissed, "Look closer, Keri, they're not what they pretend to be."

With this new illumination provided by Anger, I stared directly into each pair of eyes around the table until they looked down or away, able to see behind the masks they wore, down to the human longings they tried to conceal beneath their suits, ties, and fancy shoes. New clarity dawned on me about the roles we play and how, beneath our confident exteriors, we are not always as comfortable and secure as we may appear. For the first time in my life, I felt my own power and the Source behind it.

Calmly I listened as Anger continued, "Do not give away your power. You—the great winds that the ancient ones travel on. You—the roar of the crashing waterfalls and the wise rocks breaking it underneath. Never forget you are not only a human being, you are a cosmic being, a courageous soul who chose to travel to the Earth Realm for the unique adventure of being wholly human."

The feeling and message of Anger motivated me further until I recalled my childhood longing to choose my own adventure. How long ago that seemed! But here I was, walking the same paths again and again, paths of safety and acquiescence, willingly giving away my power to the nearest authority figure.

"But if I refuse to sign this, these people will be upset and inconvenienced," I argued.

"They are already upset and inconvenienced," Anger hissed. "Do not give them permission to influence your future. They cannot control you unless you let them. You hold the power."

"But that's not how I was raised," I insisted.

"What, that be-nice-at-all-costs nonsense? That midwestern stoicism and passive-aggressiveness? Those qualities do not reflect your true self anymore. They are designed to preserve the status quo not create change," Anger asserted.

"But isn't it nice to be nice?" I countered.

"Not at the expense of your power, Keri," Anger replied.

Abruptly, I felt something flame up from within me. I sat up a little straighter, pulled my shoulders back, narrowed my eyes, and breathed deeply. I set the pen down. "No. I won't sign this," I said in a full, calm voice. I don't recall anyone replying, perhaps because they were as surprised as I was by the change in me. I made no apology, offered no excuse or explanation, only left the room and their precious document, unsigned. I wound my way back down to my basement cubby, followed by Curiosa, collapsed in my swivel chair, and took a long drink of soda. Then I replayed the horror scene, reflecting on how I had defied those powerful people despite the fact that they could still have power over my future.

"What just happened?" Fear screamed, his tie askew and fresh burn holes riddling his pinstripe suit. "I don't understand this. I don't ever lose control!"

"Those are powerful people you're messing around with, girl, people who can destroy your future," warned Shame.

"Oh, why didn't I just sign?" I asked myself, suddenly feeling very exposed. I put my head in my hands and cried, embarrassed by what I had just done and fearful for the unknown awaiting me in Portland.

For many years, I would not associate my memories about this incident with a new empowerment and increased self-respect but rather with humiliation and self-loathing. I would quickly forget about the rush of exhilaration that had come from taking a risk to protect my true self and the subtle feeling of connection with soul that I had experienced during this episode. But, as with every forgetting, it marked the start of a later remembering of my power and who I was.

Once in Portland I hoped my old job would fade into the rearview mirror, as Minneapolis and Fargo had before that. After all, I had completed all my projects, contract or no contract. When I had sat down for my exit interview, and the human resources representative didn't bring up anything about my moving expenses or the unsigned contract, I had sighed with relief. But that relief was short-lived. Soon threatening letters on fancy stationery signed by the president were forwarded to my new address, demanding I repay my moving expenses of about $10,000 and saying that if I did not reimburse the company it would liquidate my 401k in which I'd saved a grand total of about $2,000. I didn't know if the company could do that, but, regardless, a simple trip to the mailbox became a heart-racing, palm-sweating walk that I soon delegated to Todd. Anxiety struck again, more powerful and longer lasting than ever before, and avoidance was still the only strategy I knew.

I never wrote a letter in response or sent a check. Eventually, the letters demanding repayment of my moving expenses stopped coming, and no money was taken from my 401k. Even if I had wanted to repay them I couldn't have since Todd and I had confidence, courage, and determination in spades but not much money. No matter how hard we tried, job doors were not swinging open for us in Portland. Before long our bank accounts yielded to credit accounts, which eventually also became untenable. Once, when driving home together and seeing the gas light blink on we pulled into a gas station and swiped three credit cards, discovering they were all maxed out. So we did what any reasonable person would do. We got on our hands and knees and searched for loose change under the mats, in the cup holders, on the dashboard, in the glove compartment, coming up with a dollar or two and sheepishly pouring it into the cupped hands of the attendant, who pumped some gas in our tank, after which we drove home silently in embarrassment.

Yet, despite the trying emotional and financial times, this face-down in the boardroom with people I would normally never have defied made me aware of my potential strength to do more in this world than simply uphold the status quo. One day in fifth grade, a friend with whom I was playing catch suddenly burst out laughing, saying I didn't know my own strength. I ran home crying because I believed this not to be a compliment about my strong throw but an insult directed at my intelligence. Then when my mom explained the expression to me, I felt pride and made up with my friend. Later in life I realized that my friend was right—I didn't know my own strength for a very long time. But having the courage to voice opposition to authority figures and the determination to move to Portland guided by nothing more than the continued pursuit of adventure helped me begin to know that strength.

## CHAPTER 20

# *Vasoconstriction*

AT THIS POINT IN MY LIFE, I began to think about religion as a shell game, imagining a magician, draped in a black cape, placing a single pea under one of several shells, then shuffling them and asking us to choose the shell with the pea underneath. If the shells are religions, the pea is the "right" religion, and God is the magician, how is it possible to be certain about any choice of religion? I feared for my soul.

Since leaving Fargo I'd avoided church and God except for my nightly prayer, hoping that if I just got small enough perhaps I could sneak into heaven through the eye of the needle on a technicality. But now I began to focus on my religious beliefs as a natural consequence of guilt, boredom, and disillusionment. Todd and I were living in sin, to both our parents' consternation. Neither of us had jobs to keep us busy, and we were broke. And many of my beliefs about how to be successful in life—work hard, tell the truth, trust authority figures—had shattered. I now had many urgent questions about God and religion, for which I wanted answers. Todd's religious upbringing had been the antithesis of mine. He had gone through catechism in the Catholic Church, been confirmed in the Lutheran Church, and graduated from a Christian high school. So I saw him as a knowledgeable religious insider and assumed he could handle my questions about God and religion with ease.

One Sunday afternoon at our favorite brewery, two beers in and a third on its way, I decided it was as good a time as any to get answers to these questions.

"Does God really know our thoughts?" I asked.

"Yes," Todd replied without hesitation, confirming my childhood suspicion that the sanctuary of my mind was being invaded.

"Is it a sin if you just think something?" I inquired.

"Yes," he confirmed, validating Guilt.

"Is there no other way into the Kingdom of Heaven than through Jesus?" I asked.

"No," he answered, feeding Fear.

"What happens to people in remote areas of the world who never hear of Christianity or Jesus or have their own faith?" I swallowed hard before asking my final question: "Will they go to hell?"

"Yes," he replied, apparently unconcerned about the fates of these faceless people. "That's why missionaries try to convert them."

I tried to digest this information, but questions kept piling up. What if *we* are the ones who are wrong? I thought. What if they are saying similar things about us? Could all of human existence and the afterlife in eternity really just boil down to the luck of the draw of where you are born and which shell you choose? I wondered.

I was seeking hope and security but instead grew increasingly incensed by Todd's arrogance. I wondered why he was deserving of security and not me, then Fear provided the answer: I was an outsider, and outsiders never get to feel secure.

As I kept asking questions, finally—perhaps due to the beer or perhaps because his unflappability had never been authentic—he cracked and, in a tone of mixed frustration and relief, confessed, "Dammit, Keri, this is just what I've been taught."

"But don't you want to learn more?" I further pressed his tiny window of vulnerability.

He sighed and replied, "Keri, I've had religion forced on me for so many years I don't even want to think about it, much less talk about it."

"But aren't you scared?" I asked.

"No," he assured me.

"Why not?" I pressed.

"I just believe like a child," he said.

"What's that supposed to mean?" I asked.

He expounded, "I believe in God with the innocence and trust of a child. Having faith means being submissive and meek before God, not challenging him and his every word."

I stared, dumbfounded. If we believed like a child, wouldn't we be exploring spirituality and God like a child—with curiosity? I wondered.

I was not satisfied with our conversation, nor was Curiosa. But I didn't know where to turn next. For the time being, I decided, it couldn't hurt to try it Todd's way. Unlike me, he seemed to have no sleepless nights tossing and turning over whether he'd already committed the unforgivable sin by mistake somehow. So I hoped that Christianity was, in fact, the right religion as I pointed to that shell.

"It's about time you got on God's good side, young lady. Just repeat after me, 'No god but God. No way but One,'" Guilt agreed. "Obedience will prove your worthiness, and your life will be filled with blessings."

"I don't know about that," I answered, as I watched Curiosa wane before my eyes.

❧

Initially, at least, my meek, new believe-like-a-child approach to religion—and life in general—seemed to do the trick. I experienced less anxiety as we finally both landed good-paying jobs with creative opportunities and regular raises. A year later, having been legally married in a church in my hometown, we had plans to start a family. And as we sampled some churches in Portland I sat in their pews smiling, donning the skin of a good, obedient Christian woman.

However, one day at work my meek acceptance of Christianity was challenged when a coworker and friend talked to me about Buddhism and I realized just how flimsy my church posturing had been. Joe greeted me at my work cubicle. He was someone I admired. I loved listening to his easy laugh, the sweet way he talked about his wife, and learning from his wisdom. We chatted easily for several minutes, until the conversation veered dangerously outside the lines.

"Keri, do you know much about Buddhism?" he asked.

"No," I replied, uneasily.

Everyone knew Joe was a Buddhist, but it didn't come up often.

"Tread carefully," Fear warned.

"Buddhists are sinners," Guilt reminded me. "Buddhism is the wrong shell."

"Would you like to learn a little about it over lunch sometime?" Joe asked.

"Teamwork, y'all!" Fear said, rallying my emotions. Shame slithered atop my shoulders, while Guilt talked about the sin of questioning God. But Curiosa salivated at the thought of such a conversation.

Back then I didn't know the first thing about Buddhism, and I fully accepted that Christianity was a flawed system. I was at the doorway of my journey of spiritual discovery but wouldn't embark on it until several years later. At this point in my life, fear of the unknown proved stronger than the pull of curiosity. Wearing Christianity like a loosened tie around my neck still seemed safer than taking it off.

"No, I don't think so," I whispered, tightening that tie up around my throat. "I am a Christian, and I believe like a child."

"Oh, okay," Joe said, raising his eyebrows for just a moment before shrugging and walking back to his cubicle.

My heart rate slowed down. My color returned to normal.

"Good work, team. That was a close one!" Fear said. Guilt smirked at Curiosa, both knowing her influence was dwindling.

Despite my reluctance to engage with Joe about Buddhism, this encounter with him did slightly change my view of the shell game. Knowing someone personally who had chosen a different shell, an individual with whom I had laughed, shared lunch, and occasionally debated, got me wondering if there was not one pea but many and whether there was no black-caped magician trying to trick us, only ourselves.

Today, sometimes I wonder whether if at that time in my life I had had an on/off switch allowing me to put an end to my uncomfortable feelings about being an outsider and questioner and simply accept everything I was told as the truth, I would have flipped it. Yet I know that while we can temporarily suppress our curiosity, our imagination, and our questions, we cannot ignore them forever and expect to live a fulfilling life because it is, ultimately, our capacity for curiosity that makes human life both challenging and wondrous.

## CHAPTER 21

### *Stretch Marks*

SHORTLY AFTER THE CALENDAR FLIPPED TO the new millennium, my husband and I flipped our lives upside down to begin yet again. Todd's company offered him a job in Pennsylvania, along with a promotion and a raise, giving me the chance to slip into a role I now coveted: stay-at-home mom. A businesswoman I most certainly was not; a Christian woman, questionable. But I thought I'd be a natural mother, wife, and householder able to focus on my family. As for my unresolved issues with God, I still subscribed to the "believe like a child" mantra, and, like a good wall should, it seemed to be holding back the flood of questions on the other side.

Motherhood began just as expected—with delight, confusion, sleep deprivation, and feelings of being overwhelmed. But when our daughter Cameron was three weeks old my husband and I noticed something we did not expect: she cried often, with great intensity, for hours on end. After changing, feeding, rocking, burping, bouncing, shushing, walking, and patting, all we could do was stare helplessly as she wailed with a red face and closed fists. Unable to locate the phantom tormentor anywhere on her tiny body, or pull a solution out of the wide array of baby books scattered on our living room coffee table, we ultimately sped to the emergency room for answers. Thirty minutes later, with our thrashing child lying on the exam table, the doctor bellowed his diagnosis: colic. "There is nothing you can do but allow it to pass," he said as he tucked his stethoscope back inside his coat pocket.

"How long will that take?" I asked.

"It usually dissipates at about three months of age," he replied.

Although my husband's job had provided the financial means for me to stay home with our infant daughter, this privilege now came with a price tag—long hours alone with a colicky baby while work kept my husband away for all but a few waking hours. With no friends or relatives around to help, I soon felt more isolated and incompetent than I ever had in an office cubicle. Small logs of resentment toward my husband began stacking up inside me. I didn't dare acknowledge them since ingratitude was surely a sin in God's eyes.

"Let's see, we've still got dinner to prepare, a diaper to change, your husband's dry cleaning to pick up," Fear said one afternoon, ticking off items on the day's to-do list, slithering up and down my body, sending me chills, headaches, and digestive pain.

"You should be better at juggling all these tasks, not to mention child care; after all, a woman's place is in the home," Guilt chided.

Images of cuddling my cooing, adorable infant proved to be only daydreams. Sometimes, with no particular destination in mind, I would take Cameron for car rides, subscribing to the common belief that all babies sleep in cars. But apparently my daughter hadn't read the manuals. When I stayed home, I would try buckling her in her car seat and placing it on the running dryer, but rather than soothing her it usually frightened her. Ultimately, only one combination worked consistently: placing her in her baby swing and turning the vacuum cleaner on high. Her eyes would gloss over, she'd fall asleep, and I would run to wash clothes, fix myself lunch, or go to the bathroom before she'd wake with a wail and we'd begin again.

"Even a vacuum makes a better mother!" Shame would admonish me.

During these weeks of her colic, I never met anyone who had struggled so much with motherhood—or at least anyone who admitted to such struggles. All I felt was the judgment of my emotions and that of "better" moms wondering why I didn't soothe my crying child sitting in her car seat or stroller, or, if I was holding her, thinking I must be hurting her. When I did confide in others about our long, hard days or how I dreamed of quiet days reading a book and enjoying a glass of wine, people would sometimes say, "Oh, the poor baby! You know, I had a friend whose baby had colic, and she found that [fill-in-the-blank] worked for her."

"Yes, I tried that," I would reply with a tight smile and an obligatory thank you.

One day I admitted sheepishly to my mom over the phone,

"I can stand it for about five hours, but then I just can't do it anymore."

"Put her down then," she advised, calmly. "She'll be okay."

I placed my crying daughter in her crib, snuck outside, sat on my front step, and closed the door behind me. Fear, Guilt, and Shame traded remarks: "What if it's something worse than colic?" "She needs a loving, attentive, patient mother, not someone who walks away." "You should already know how to do this."

Ultimately, as the doctor had said, after about three months we observed an evident reduction in the intensity and length of her crying spells. Then she became a happy, adventurous baby showering us with smiles, ready to take on the world with the same vigor she had previously funneled into crying.

Meanwhile, I had been experiencing a growing list of physical symptoms too obvious to ignore. While I wanted to embrace Cameron's new enthusiasm and not address the bodily symptoms that had been piling up like dirty laundry—fatigue, cold sweats, chest tightness, chronic digestive pain, insomnia, low libido—I feared that something serious and maybe irreversible was happening to me. Finally, I shared my symptoms with my doctor. But he glanced at my list, took my blood pressure, checked my pulse, listened to my heart, poked my body, and concluded, "Well, there doesn't seem to be anything physically wrong. Maybe you've just been experiencing some stress."

Three weeks later familiar red circles which bled into large masses appeared on my skin, for me tangible proof that there was, in fact, something wrong with me. I went to an allergist, who, after blood tests proved that my hives were not a reaction to a known allergen, prescribed Benadryl for the itching and Prednisone to suppress or minimize the outbreaks.

"You'll want to use Prednisone with caution," he said. "And don't stop taking it, even after your hives go away. You have to step down from it. There are some side—"

"I know all about Prednisone," I interrupted. "My mom has been on it for years after a kidney transplant." My mom had told me about the side effects of Prednisone—a possibility of weakening bones, weight gain, swelling, high blood pressure, and mood changes. I didn't want anything to do with Prednisone, but I also couldn't effectively take care of my family with hives plaguing me. My solution was to allow the hives to build up each day to the point of intolerance then, frustrated, slam down a Prednisone.

My midwestern roots had proved their ability to bend during my youthful travels, but after facing infant colic and chronic hives their natural flexibility, like my body's, wore out and snapped my family and me back to Minnesota with a force reminiscent of a mother pulling her delinquent child home by the ear. Minnesota, which I had left five years earlier because of a job transfer and to escape the cold and bleakness of winter, welcomed me home, making me feel safe again. So I was not surprised when, once our family's move was complete, my hives, which had lasted over six months, faded. Ignoring my doctor's warnings, I threw out the rest of my Prednisone, followed by my birth control pills since my husband and I had agreed that the odds against a second colicky baby were astronomically in our favor. But the odds beat us, and within a few weeks of our second daughter Kelsey's birth we noticed the telltale signs of colic.

Kelsey's colic was like Cameron's in many ways. However, Kelsey cried with a desperate expression on her face and at a volume that turned heads in grocery stores, parking lots, and restaurants, and stopped people on the sidewalk in front of our house, likely pondering if they should call the police. Her screams prompted us to race twice to the emergency room, where she was always pronounced healthy and doctors encouraged me to be patient.

This situation made all my most pronounced emotions battle for power, plus one I had not usually allowed myself to acknowledge: Anger. Anger unleashed a fiery rant: "It's not fair! What the hell did I do to deserve this torture? Can't anyone get some fucking peace and quiet around here just for one day?" Not knowing yet how to deal with this brutal, profanity-speaking force within me, I rolled my eyes and silently raged at "better" moms and other concerned citizens who dared to say, "Poor child." I roared at my husband for his inability to "fix" this problem when he could fix everything else. I hurled imaginary rocks at doctors who fed me lines like, "Don't worry, it'll only last three months," seemingly blind to the fact that every day with a colicky baby aged my body by a week. I was incensed at glowing mothers on the covers of my parenting books, the dusty bookshelves and unmade beds, and the nice day outside that I couldn't enjoy.

"There must be a way to blockade Anger," Fear whispered, "Keep him locked up inside. Then over time he will likely lose fire power and convert to something less risky—and if we're lucky, less vulgar."

"Like Self-Loathing or Depression?" Guilt suggested, drooling over the idea.

Fear frowned and replied, "I don't know, Guilt, but we must try something before Anger burns any other point of view to ashes!"

From childhood to college life to corporate life to married life, I had been down, but no one and nothing had yet knocked me out. However, two colicky infants had brought me to my knees, humbled and light-years away from the warrior's independence and confidence that had characterized my earlier years. Confused by the various perspectives of my battling emotions and exhausted, I finally had to admit I needed help—from my mother.

"She's going to see what a horrible mother you've turned out to be!" Shame and Fear said in unison.

Yet despite their warnings I asked my mom if my daughters and I could live with her until the colic subsided. Luckily, Fargo was only a four-hour drive from our Minnesota home. A couple days later my mom opened her door to allow in her sleep-deprived daughter and her let's-just-call-them-spirited granddaughters. She greeted my girls with kisses, hugs, and playful talk. Watching her express such spontaneous emotion with her guard down gave me unexpected pleasure and made me hope that she had cooed over me like that when I was little. My mom, in the same take-charge way she had once shoved pillows into broken windows to protect against hail, organized my overstuffed closet of struggle and strife into a single drawer of perspective. Her poised manner and level-headed tone said to me: Let's take care of this crisis now, we can panic/cry/get angry later, just as she had behaved during the storm earlier in her life. As if in a three-legged race, my mom and I hobbled to the finish line. During these weeks under my mother's wing, I learned resilience and perseverance. As her daughter, these qualities had sometimes seemed stoic and unfeeling, but as an adult and mother myself I saw them anew as wise, capable, and strong.

When reflecting on those early years, I hypothesize that my girls were colicky because their powerfully charged souls simply couldn't abide the helplessness of infant bodies, or that they were trying to inform me, through the language of colic, that they had not chosen their human lives simply to make me proud but had their own hopes, dreams, and life purposes. Certainly their colic blew away a belief I had held that having children would be like making instant coffee: add water, mix, get happiness. The error of this belief lay within how I had entered motherhood—placing my potential for happiness in their tiny laps, thinking they would make me whole in a way I had not been able to do for myself. If their infancies had been easier, I might have continued living vicariously through them, using their behavior and accomplishments in the world as a reflection of not only my parenting skills but my own value as an individual. However, my girls, seemingly still connected to their Source of life, would only accept a genuine love. Maybe because of their colicky beginnings my love for my children then and now is not the instinctual love I had once imagined mothers had but more of a cultivated love that engulfs me every day. Ultimately, my girls saved me from a lifetime of believing that conditional love is all I deserve or all I'm capable of giving.

## *Depression's Call to Duty*

WITH COLORING WANDS PICKED OUT OF A BOX, I paint the landscape and all of us at the precipice in rich hues. The landscape is now more colorful, detailed, and imbued with warmth, inviting more wildlife to join us and gardens to spontaneously grow. A pond now sparkles in shades of blue, nicely complementing the blue of my eyes, and thin strips of chestnut and mahogany accent my hair. Curiosa's silver fur is now trimmed with black to match her nose, and her cool, silver-colored eyes have warmed to a dark chocolate shade.

When I'm satisfied with the new appearance of my surroundings, I snap my fingers to erase my efforts and begin again. I brush the branches and twigs that form the settee with bold color. Snap. I paint the oak trees with rainbow stripes and circles. Snap. I turn the pond into chalky pastels. Snap. I paint Rasa's tote bag as a not-too-shabby replica of Vincent van Gogh's *Starry Night*. Snap. My artistic play reminds me that creativity is not about perfection or permanence but about exploration and enjoyment, something I hope to remember in my next life.

"How about a refresher?" Rasa asks, offering me a glass of Stardust Chardonnay. "A whole afternoon lies ahead of us yet." I accept the wine, ready to take a break from coloring.

But then a ghostly, desperate-looking creature suddenly appears in the landscape and darkens all my fresh color. I quickly pluck out the glossiest, most colorful wand from the box and chase after the creature, scribbling hurriedly, trying to prevent it from subduing all colors in its path. But as quickly as I reintroduce colors the creature mutes them in a single pass. Finally, the dismal creature collapses on the settee, and I return, gasping, to Rasa's side.

"That is Depression demonstrating the power of his cloak of empty calories," she murmurs.

"So he will be taking this trip with me?" I say, assuming that this is the reason for his arrival here. Rasa nods.

"I remember Depression," I muse. "It was because of him that some pictures in my travel scrapbook would not come back to life no matter how hard I pressed on them." My energy sinks as I recall how in so many human lives Depression hampered my progress and stole my power. "I will vanquish that demon this time," I vow. While my words are forceful, my voice, clearly affected by Depression, is monotone.

Rasa, her usual colorful clothing now black and white, grimaces, reflecting her own past encounters with Depression. "The difficulty of chasing him down in soul form has now been made apparent. You cannot hope that in a human body you will have a better chance of keeping him at bay, much less defeating him, through a warrior's means only. You must consider a more creative approach to Depression, because if you are to be an advocate for emotions you cannot exclude him. You will have better results if you view Depression as a teacher not an enemy," she counsels.

"A teacher?" I glance at the gray shadow clinging to the settee and wince. "What does Depression have to teach? It seems that all he does is steal from life, not add to it," I insist.

"Mentors appear in many shapes and colors," my soul friend continues patiently. "There will come a time when he will entice you to take cover inside his cloak of empty calories. But as you're considering his offer, if you take a moment to recall all that is good in your life, that which brings a feeling of happiness or a sense of well-being, you can instead use his visit to trigger yet another new beginning."

I contemplate Depression, as I have never before associated him with fresh, new beginnings but rather with painful endings. His coal-colored, batlike eyes stare back at me, his cloak of empty calories waving enticingly in the breeze, as I wonder, with trepidation, how large a role he will play in my next life and if I can learn to view him as a teacher with a unique purpose in human life.

## CHAPTER 23

### *New Skin*

ONE POST-COLIC SUMMER AFTERNOON IN FALL 2002, upon receiving a mommy time-out I felt the tug of an old, familiar love: books. I went to a bookstore with the expectation of immediate pleasure in perusing but felt nothing. I'm just a little out of practice, I reassured myself, having only read pregnancy and baby books for the last several years. I began a more deliberate hunt. I scanned the floor for the "accidental book drop," the shelves for the "misfiled book," the new releases for a juicy vampire novel to sink my teeth into. I held several different books in my hands, waiting for the bodily sensation that meant "Yes, read me." But nothing happened. Soon I slunk out empty-handed.

Then I scheduled an appointment with my doctor. I walked her through a list of ongoing physical symptoms, ending with the experience that worried me most—my book-shopping failure.

"Would you consider taking a test for depression?" she asked, compassionately.

Depression? I was taken aback. To me, depression was something that happened to other people; surely ambitious, intelligent, capable women like me did not get depression. But after I agreed to take the test reality set in as the quiz tally rose higher and higher.

"It's your own fault for not putting God first in your life," Guilt chided.

"You are a weakling," Shame added.

I walked out of the doctor's office with a prescription for Zoloft in one hand and a crumpled tissue in the other.

Once home, I curled up in our leather rocking chair, with my arms hugging my knees, feeling the full power of depression. Through cloudy eyes, I looked around at our quiet house in the suburbs—one on which we could pay the mortgage each month, with money left over for food, clothing, insurance, incidentals, even extra to design rooms myself in warm, soothing palettes—and wondered if I'd missed a turn somewhere. As I took in an otherwise heartwarming scene, my appreciation was interrupted by thoughts undermining my sense of self-worth. Movement, beauty, and warmth adorned the home (I failed at corporate life). Pictures of my happy, healthy family hung on the walls (I'm thirty now, and what have I accomplished?). My husband and I had rebounded from the stress of our girls' colic (I failed at being a good mom). Our community was expanding (thanks solely to my husband's extroverted personality). My husband had settled into a great career path that made it unnecessary for me to get a "real" job again (I'm not even putting my education to use).

"My dear malnourished child," Depression said. "Withdraw into me, I will fill your emptiness. Stop seeking meaning or purpose. They are fairy tales. This world is an ugly, unjust place where only rejection and disappointment await. But many humans shelter themselves inside my cloak of empty calories, and so can you." Depression's offer tasted like a cool drink of water in the desert.

"Immerse yourself in the lighter side of life," Depression continued, "television shows, movies, food, drink, shopping, whatever distances you from the world's pain. Let go, surrender, give in to the sweet pull of my cloak of empty calories." Depression's offer felt like the way a night shields us from the harshness of light.

"Best of all, my child, I can protect you from feelings of anxiety, which will continue to plague your life. I can assure you that a lifetime with me is safer than a lifetime with anxiety."

His offer was tempting. But before I could totally surrender to Depression I ventured further into the depths of my mind. There, as if touching an electric fence, I came across a live-wire emotion that was bitter, and sparking with pain and unfairness: Anger.

Damn it, I thought. No one had followed the breadcrumb trail to success more faithfully than I had. No one had believed in the promises of the world more than I had. No one had tried harder to follow the rules than I had!

"Ignore Anger!" Depression shouted. "He has nothing valuable to add to your life. I'll snuff him out, too. I can give you the quiet life you want."

But it wasn't a quiet life I wanted; I wanted my mind, heart, and lifestyle to peacefully coexist, though at the time I didn't know how to differentiate between peace and quiet. I pounded my fists on the arms of the rocking chair, an act of resistance that temporarily silenced Depression.

"Ah yes, remember fists of fury?" Anger growled.

I did remember. Before we had children, my husband and I had taken kickboxing classes and opted to participate in light sparring sessions on Saturday mornings. One time our young trainer pitted my husband and me against each other. To be fair, my husband's side of the story is that I told him not to go easier on me than he would on anyone else. But even if that was what I had said I'm sure I didn't mean it. He thrust his stark white glove toward my nose so fast it left me no time to react or block. The impact stung on many levels. I struck back with what he later called "fists of fury" while he held his gloves steady in front of his face. The trainer separated us. I glared at my husband, sweat dripping down my face, fire and aliveness radiating from my eyes.

I chuckled at this memory. But it wasn't the one that got me out of my rocking chair and away from Depression's enticement.

Another memory came to me. Years before, when trying to conceive our first child, I had visited a doctor for fertility medication, and, even as he prescribed the medication for me, he suggested I also try yoga classes. Yoga wasn't for athletes like myself, I thought, as I pictured old men in loincloths sitting still for hours. But once I got home Curiosa had raced to-

ward a pile of junk mail on our kitchen table and brought me
a brochure from a community education center advertising a
six-week course called Introduction to Yoga. "Okay, what have
I got to lose?" I had asked. In that yoga class, I had experienced
a new relationship with my body—deep relaxation, sweet con-
tentedness, regeneration, and a fresh outlook. I'd walked out
of those classes with my steps lighter than at any other time
during the week. But by the time the six weeks ended I was
pregnant, and we moved to Pennsylvania, where I was soon
immersed in diapers and colic, forgetting all about yoga.

My body responded to this second memory in a way that
I knew was affirmative—my fingers tingled, and my heart was
lighter. I turned to tell this news to Curiosa, who had loved
our yoga classes, only to realize that she was not by my side.
No wonder I could find no books that I wanted to explore, I
thought. Vowing I would find Curiosa and regain my passion
and love of life, I rose from the rocking chair, walked into the
kitchen, opened a fat Yellow Pages amongst sippy cups and
stray Cheerios, and flipped to the "Y" section.

Depression was duly prepared to protect me from my pain,
cover up my frustrations, and sugarcoat my disappointments
with his cloak of empty calories. He was fully capable of keeping my anger and anxiety hidden, too. But he could only feign
happiness, peace, joy, and pleasure, while some deeper part of
me still believed I could access the genuine emotions. Even
better than a good book, yoga, I believed, could put me on a path
to a lifetime of peace, and maybe even joy.

# PART IV

## Absorption and Assimilation

✎

*Like a sponge,
the skin absorbs the necessary nutrients, oxygen,
and moisture to stay supple and strong.
However, there is a limit to what the skin can absorb.
If the skin is lathered with too many products,
even if they are of good quality
and used with good intentions,
they may create a buildup that can become toxic.*

### CHAPTER 24

## *Process of Soul Embodiment*

RASA TAKES MY HAND and pulls me toward the pond. Along its sandy shore is a red-checkered blanket with a white wicker picnic basket in the center. "Lunch has arrived, and wait till you see the feast that awaits us!" she says, gesturing toward the basket. "Fried chicken, mashed potatoes, sweet corn, radishes—some of Grandma's pleasures from the Earth Realm, made just for you."

I haven't desired a meal since my return to the Soul Realm. But suddenly my stomach rumbles, and I sit down cross-legged on the blanket, open the basket, and inhale the pleasurable scent of home-cooked Earth Realm food.

"Come on, wild one!" adds Rasa, welcoming my wolf with a pat. "Don't think I forgot about you!" Curiosa sniffs at her meal, a book entitled *Fostering Reunions between Humans and Their Lost Soul Animals, One Soulfully Crafted Match at a Time* by Rights Advocate for Soul Animals, aka Rasa. Curiosa devours it in a single bite.

"So that is your project! You are building an animal shelter for soul animals who are neglected or lost!" I exclaim before I dive into buttery mashed potatoes.

"Exactly," she says with a proud smile. "And while the animals rejuvenate I will campaign on their behalf to their human owners through various means. In my research, I have found that memory is a particularly effective way to awaken humans to the gradual loss of their wholeness."

Questions pop into my mind. "Why is this needed now? What services will you provide? And, most importantly, where will it be located?" I ask.

With her mouth showing fierce determination instead of her usual fun-loving smile, Rasa explains, "In other Earth Realm times, and in many places where the earth is still revered and humanity less tiered, humans not only respect their soul animals but actively seek their companionship. However, with so much power and influence currently going toward sustaining the material world, very little energy remains for the mysterious inner world. This has made soul animals endangered. Their great gifts remain unused, left to spoil like unpicked fruit, and the animals themselves are suffering, many starving or dying."

I give Curiosa a reassuring pat and remark, "Humans. They search the whole planet for a soul mate, never realizing they have one already in their soul animals."

"This is an important truth you speak," my innovative friend continues, her tone resolute. "At the shelter the animals, birds, and reptiles will be fed, bathed, and kept strong and healthy until their humans are ready to reclaim them. As for your final question," she says, her tone brightening, "do you remember the bridge that connects the material realm to the spiritual realm, the one that humans cross when they're seeking deeper dimensions and higher truth?"

I nod.

She continues, "I am setting up shop just on the spiritual side of that bridge. Humans seeking to reunite with their soul animals—which usually indicates they are seeking a richer life and are willing to take some risks to that end—need to venture at least a few steps into the infinite, timeless world of the spirit. This single visit may lead to more, which could inspire other humans to follow the path over the bridge, and eventually trigger a much-needed spiritual revolution in the Earth Realm."

"Which could result in a healthier planet with more mindful, compassionate humans," I add. "Your plan is quite profound, Rasa! How did you think of it?" I ask, impressed by her ingenuity.

She shrugs and replies, "I saw the need, I felt called, and, in a soul blink, it became my personal passion and purpose. Now I am so immersed in this work that I know I will not cease until all humans are reunited with their soul animals."

Inspiration jolts through my soul body. "I understand. That is what my eternal search for the Great Truth feels like—a calling, something I can never give up," I say.

Rasa pushes her jeweled glasses further up the bridge of her nose and, in a serious tone, says, "Then it is time we talk about the process of embodiment and how to communicate with your ego because without embodiment, and the strong communication embodiment would cultivate between you and your ego, your search for the Great Truth will likely be side-lined in favor of following your ego's desires for validation from a fickle world."

At the mere sound of the word *embodiment*, a thrill rushes through me.

"First, my dear, let us talk about what embodiment means. Do you still have those Earth Realm dictionaries at your disposal?" Rasa asks.

Grinning, I conjure up a few dictionaries and websites and browse through them. "The dictionaries define embodiment as the 'representation or expression of something in tangible form.' So under that definition is not this radish embodied? Or a book? Or even a rock?" I ask.

Rasa tilts her head and replies, "I would assume so. But there must be something more specific."

I search for definitions of soul embodiment rather than simply embodiment and find decent ones. "This one says, 'Soul embodiment means allowing the soul to fully incarnate into the body.' And another says embodiment means 'opening to the highest levels of experience of the true self.' Still none fully describes the feeling state of embodiment. Perhaps I shall create my own definition," I say.

"I was hoping you would do that," replies Rasa, who with a snap of her fingers sends the dictionaries away.

I pace slowly as I reflect upon my previous lifetimes. I recall that embodiment does not occur naturally upon incarnation, nor is a soul promised this experience in the course of any human lifetime. Soul embodiment requires several things: an invitation from the ego; a shared commitment to growing consciousness; an open dialogue between soul and ego; and a willingness to feel and express emotion. I close my eyes and speak of embodiment from these remembered experiences rather than from some memorized definition: "Soul embodiment is an authenticity of feeling. It means to live in alignment with the naked truth of human experience and be aware of its impact on all layers, visible and invisible, of the human body. Soul embodiment means to feel without boundaries, discrimination, or judgment all that is available to be felt in each moment. It is a borderless, skinless experience in which the soul is no longer contained within the body and mind, but the body and mind are contained within the soul." I open my eyes.

"That is a good start," Rasa replies, nodding. "Tell me more about how embodiment feels."

Again I reach back into my previous life experiences, this time searching for the feeling state of embodiment. Deciding to show her as well as tell her, I plant my feet firmly on the ground, and then let my upper body, arms, and head sway in the breeze, mimicking an Earth Realm tree and then describe the feeling by saying, "When I am embodied, there is no denial of any part of myself, no need to split anything off from the whole, no suppression or avoidance of my truth. When I am embodied, I can speak my truth, express my creativity, feel connected to myself and others, and sense my innate belonging and duty to the planet."

182 ~ Embodying Soul

"Remember, too," Rasa adds, letting her body bend like a tree playing with the breeze, "that embodiment is not a reward or a final destination, but a feeling state that often comes and goes in a lifetime. The more you experience it, the longer you can sustain that feeling."

She catches my hand in the air, twirls me toward her, then continues, "I must offer a word of caution. Sometimes, in the Earth Realm, humans speak of something called enlightenment. While enlightenment, like embodiment, will lead to many great truths and an authentic life, only embodiment will ensure that you stay connected to the Earth and its inhabitants while drawing down the greatest gifts of the Soul Realm. And only embodiment will enable you to do the work you, Sëri, are intending to do in the Earth Realm with integrity, truth, and trust."

"Truly it is embodiment that I long for in this upcoming human life," I say, as I cross my hands at the wrists and place them over my heart. "Then I can both assist in reawakening the inner worlds of spirit and magic and bring people back together in community through story." I add with a wink, "Perhaps I could even help topple a few of those hierarchies of power we've discussed."

Rasa laughs. "Surely that is something you can do, Sëri. Which is why I wrote you a list of guidelines to the process of soul embodiment," Rasa says, grinning mischievously as she offers me a piece of paper folded in thirds.

"I know," she says, flipping a wrist dismissively after catching my teasing glance, "I don't usually write lists—especially for things that are, by nature, far more complicated than can be reflected in a list. But some souls, like you, prefer lists, and it is important that every soul has access to this critical information in whatever format suits them best. Please consider these points as only general guidelines rather than orders."

With anticipation, I open the list she has given me, composed in her graceful, ornate handwriting.

### Process of Soul Embodiment
### by Rasa

1. Use your creativity to assure the ego of your existence and that you, Serene Voyager, will not be marginalized to the role of silent witness or be someone from whom the ego can garner occasional support.

2. Use the magic and creativity of your common soul animal, Curiosa, to assist in communications with the ego. The more devoted she becomes to this soul animal, the thinner the veil between her and you will become and the easier communication will be.

3. Guide the ego toward experiences that will take her deep inside her body and mind to feel and reflect, for body awareness, mindful reflection, and soul embodiment are codependent and evolve simultaneously.

4. The language of emotions is the mutual

language of soul and ego; so in listening to her emotions the ego will move nearer to you. The more the ego feels, the more embodied you will become. The more embodied you become, the more she will feel. Therefore, encourage the ego not to suppress, ignore, or disown emotions but to instead acknowledge the right of all emotions to exist. Emotional suppression, like a wound that is covered but never examined or cleansed, will drive experiences and memories deeper into the subconscious, where they will fester. Once brought into consciousness, fears and insecurities will lose their power, and what is meant to be released will fall away, while what is meant to remain will be enriched.

5. Strengthen communication with the ego by establishing sensations that mean yes and no, and communicating this code to the ego from an early age. Then, as the ego invites you further into her life, refine this system of communication. Communication between the ego and soul can be strengthened by doing the following:

- Using synchronicities, signs, and gut feelings linked with events to encourage the ego's awakening.

- Letting the ego hear what she needs to hear through her teachers, guides, and mentors.

• Using moments of silence, stillness, or height-
ened awareness, when the ego is receptive, to
communicate to her, as such moments are
open doorways for dialogue. Over time, she will
understand that she can dialogue with you
more directly and consciously.

6. Remind the ego that letting go is a natural
process that cannot be rushed and that failure to let
go of anything will eventually result in running
out of room to absorb new things. Remind her to
move mindfully in the world, doing just one thing
at a time, letting change be integrated before moving
on to the next thing.

7. Assure the ego that the awakening occurring
during soul embodiment is irreversible, despite the
fact that egos can deny, deflect, and project. Let the
ego know that while the process of soul embodiment
is challenging it is no more challenging than living
a life without soul. And remind her that she is
loved perpetually by you and by the creator of the
universe—and that nothing she does can cause her to
lose that love.

After reading this list, I look at its author, her fingers in-
terlaced, thumbs rolling nervously, and say, "Rasa, this list is
most impressive."

"Thank you," she says, blushing.

"But I do have a question. How will I remember these guidelines once I cross the River of Forgetting?" I ask.

She replies, "Through reading, hearing, or otherwise sensing this knowledge in the Earth Realm—via teachers, books, pop culture—you will have a feeling of having accessed it before. You shall know the truth by its resonance in your body. Now let us return to the precipice, shall we?"

Together we close the picnic basket and roll up the blanket. With Curiosa right behind us, we stroll back to the precipice.

"Sëri," Rasa says, placing her hands on her hips and nodding in mock sternness toward the nearly empty suitcase waiting on the settee, "we had better focus on packing the soul tools needed for your next life."

## CHAPTER 25

## *Overdue Nourishment*

My first yoga teacher, Maryann, a lively and ageless woman with dark, shoulder-length hair set off by a wide, white smile, greeted me at her Monday night yoga class. She led Curiosa and me down steep wooden steps into a darkened basement, where I saw immobile bodies bordering the room in L shapes.

Maryann whispered, "This is called Legs up the Wall Pose. I will show you how to do it."

She folded two wool blankets into the size of a thick pillow and butted them against the wall, then indicated that I should sit sideways on top so that my left shoulder and hip touched the wall. She helped me swing my legs up and lie back, so that my hips were elevated on the blankets and the bottoms of my bare feet were facing the ceiling. She tied a D-ring yoga strap around my thighs and tightened it until holding my legs up became effortless. She asked me to turn my palms upward alongside my body, then she placed an eye pillow over my eyes.

Finally, she covered me with a soft blanket and advised me to remain as still as possible.

Paradoxically, as Maryann covered me with a blanket at that first yoga class, layers of self-protection lifted off me, and I almost cried from the caring touch of another human being, wondering when someone had last approached me so tenderly without wanting anything in return. My life at that point revolved around my young children, and, despite my love for them, it was all-consuming work. My husband was traveling a lot for his job, and when he was home and gave me attention I assumed it was only because he wanted sex.

Now, as I lay there, I could feel my heart contracting and expanding, and in the silence thought I could even hear it. I heard Fear and Guilt arguing in my mind about why I was wasting my time doing this when I could be home catching up on chores. But I heard Anger push back, saying, "Just one moment of peace. Is that too much to ask!" It was intense and powerful, reminding me of the time my family and I had eaten bananas purchased from a roadside vendor in Costa Rica, agreeing ecstatically that every other banana we'd ever had in our lives had been a poor replica of the real thing.

The following weeks I returned to Maryann's class longing to place my body in Legs up the Wall Pose, lie in the darkened silence, and feel more, although I couldn't yet explain why. The classes followed what became a predictable routine. After leaving us alone for fifteen or twenty minutes in Legs up the Wall Pose, Maryann would sit on a cushion in front of the fireplace; break the silence reverently, like breaking Communion bread;

and say, "Watch your breath. It was always there, you just weren't paying attention to it. Now you know more about your breath than when you walked into the room." So I'd note the way my breath entered me effortlessly; slipped down into my belly, which rose and expanded; then exited, a little warmer after the journey. Soon it felt like my breath followed the shape of an oval rather than an in-and-out or up-and-down pattern. On my inhale, my breath traced the curves along the back of my spine, then it curved under my tailbone, ready to move up the front of my spine as I exhaled. I had never experienced the subtleties of my breath, my life force, and I found it fascinating.

Finally, Maryann would lead us out of Legs up the Wall Pose one step at a time until we pushed ourselves up to a comfortable seated position, by saying, "First, bring awareness to your hands and feet. Just imagine your hands and feet moving. Now follow through and move your hands and feet. Do just one thing at a time. Now let your knees fall down into your chest. Wait. Integrate that much change." The concepts of one thing at a time, mindful movement, integrating change sounded both foreign to me and also strangely familiar, like I'd heard them somewhere before.

Then Maryann would lead us through sixty minutes of classical yoga poses, each guided by a simple principle she called "action within the form," explaining that this was her "innovative approach to teaching the same old poses." Under her guidance, a pose was never finished. Instead, we practiced surrendering, twisting, extending, and folding within each one. Along the way, she soaked each yoga pose in philosophy like tea leaves in hot water. By the time my body was fully settled in a Downward Facing Dog Pose, I understood that I was not there primarily to stretch the backs of my legs but was learning what descending consciousness felt like by pressing my heels into the floor and what ascending consciousness felt like by reaching my spine and fingers into the world. During poses such as Triangle Pose, Maryann encouraged us to "lengthen the dark side," inviting us to bring our shadow sides to the light of awareness, knowing that we had no chance of changing anything we wouldn't first acknowledge. Her teachings, dancing equally with eternal wisdom and earthly knowing, showed us an embodied way to live—with our feet grounded, our hearts open, our gaze steady, and our arms extended out to the world, very much like a tree.

One Monday Maryann said, "Pay attention to your thoughts. They were always there, you just weren't paying attention. Now you know more about your thoughts than when you walked into the room." Watching my thoughts, I was surprised at how active my mind was, even while my body was perfectly still in Legs up the Wall Pose. I wondered how I could not have noticed that a Shakespearean play was constantly going on in my mind with the same cast of characters, the same plot, day in and day out. I had questions wanting answers.

I opened the door to my mind and tiptoed inside. I was shocked to discover its state of chaos—like the aftermath of a drunken fraternity party. My unsupervised emotions were drunk on and addicted to their own beliefs. My thoughts were a maze of false starts and botched endings. Outdated promises to myself were written, like graffiti, on the walls. I picked up one of several empty bottles from the floor, turned to the snake hiding in a corner wearing a pinstriped suit, and demanded, "What was in this bottle, Fear?"

"Um, that was ambition, Keri. We concocted it when you were young so you could be successful," he answered with false confidence.

"Well, I'm clearly out of it, now, aren't I?" I accused, tipping the bottle upside down.

"Yes. Well, Guilt was trying to rustle up some more," Fear insisted, pointing to Guilt.

"No, Fear, I don't want any more ambition. It's poison for me," I said. "Don't we have a healthier elixir, like self-love or even self-respect?" I searched around, but except for a few scraps of praise scribbled on old report cards there wasn't much in my mind that could be called self-anything.

"No—not yet, Keri," Fear admitted, gulping. "We emotions can't make those things for you. You need to make them yourself. And if you ever make any compassion—"

"Compassion for you, Fear? Ha, that'll never happen," I assured him. "You don't deserve it after the mess you've made in here."

"I was only trying my best," Fear insisted, hanging his head.

I walked out, promising to come back soon to start cleaning the place up. While a bit horrified by what I had found in my mind, I was also oddly fascinated. I felt like finally, in my own way, I was beginning that course in psychology I'd always longed to take—with myself as my first client. Like a wheat stalk standing tall in the path of an oncoming combine, I knew this path of yoga would transform my mind and life, and I could barely wait.

## CHAPTER 26

*Soul Tools*

EVEN IN A SETTING AS MAGICAL AS THE SOUL REALM, suitcases do not pack themselves. So with my soul friend across from me, a steaming mug of peppermint tea at my right hip, a list and a pencil at my left, I tie my long hair into a low ponytail and get to work. An array of potential items sits between us: ancient wisdom tools and commonsense accessories; gems to realign each energy chakra along the spine of the human body; scents and sounds to awaken memories or inner knowledge.

Rasa reaches into the pile to pick out the first item. "What in soulnations?" I ask, noting that this item seems nothing more than a glass comb.

"Look closer," she instructs, beaming.

I turn the comb over in my hands and brush its sharp, fine teeth against my palm. Its stunning beauty belies its strength. Etched into its glass handle are the words *neti neti*, Sanskrit for "not this, not that." I exclaim, "Oh, this comb is not for hair, is it?"

"That is the Comb of Discernment, for use in searching for the Great Truth," Rasa replied. "If there is a crumb of truth within life's sandboxes of uncertainty, the comb will pick it out. If there is a kernel of wisdom buried under the rocks of convention, the comb will rake it up. When you place an item, such as a philosophical statement or a piece of advice, under the discerning teeth of that comb, the item's true nature will be revealed, and you will know whether or not it is for you.

This makes perfect sense since *neti neti* is a Vedic truth-seeking method of trying on and taking off, masking and un-masking until the fit is right.

The next item Rasa pulls from the pile is a heavy glass mir-ror with the phrase "Love yourself first" encircling the handle in gold lettering.

"Ah, the Mirror of Self-Love!" I exclaim, my eyes igniting as I take it in my hands.

"Exactly. While the effectiveness of the Comb of Dis-cernment cannot be discounted, over time combing through convictions, beliefs, and values can erode one's sense of self. Stripping away at yourself while not building anything stronger in its place is a dangerous proposition. To maintain health and balance, the comb must be paired with the mirror; ambitious truth-seeking must be paired with patient self-love."

I peer into the mirror, seeing an image of my ego in her mid-thirties, with long, thin bronze eyebrows; high, curved cheek-bones; and heart-shaped pink lips—all features familiar from the last time I saw my ego in the boardroom, except for her short hair.

"My hair is short! When did that happen?" I ask.

Rasa peeks over my shoulder and explains, "At some point along her spiritual journey, your ego makes that choice. Any hairstylist in the Earth Realm will tell you that how a woman wears her hair often reflects the changes occurring inside her. In your ego's case, her short hair is demonstrating both her willingness to be seen in the world and her choice to release the old and embrace the new," explains Rasa.

I look into the mirror again. My lips curl into a smile, and at first the image in the mirror looks surprised but then smiles back, her eyes growing soft. "She was slim last time I saw her but not this thin! Is she healthy?" I ask.

"She has begun a vegetarian diet and is exercising quite a lot," Rasa answers. "So her body has changed. As for her health—well, I will tell you that what she hungers for most cannot come from any physical food because what she hungers for most is for someone to look at her the way you are looking at her right now."

I make silly faces at the woman. She laughs quietly, and as she does she brings a hand up to cover her mouth. I hope one day to encourage her to feel more self-confidence so she can throw her head back and laugh freely without covering her mouth to contain her jubilance.

"There are no shortcuts to self-love," Rasa says, as she watches the two of us play in the mirror. "It takes time, patience, and gentleness to cultivate it," Rasa emphasizes.

I wave good-bye to my ego, and thank my soul friend for the gift and the information.

"You are most welcome," she answers. "Now, one final item." She pulls from the pile what appears to be a pen.

"This is the Pen of Reflection," she explains. "Although such a tool is often employed in the making of lists and reminders, or even mindless doodles, this one transforms into a magical communication tool when used in combination with the human journal, encouraging expression of the emotions and the body's sensations in the service of greater self-awareness. It is possible—indeed likely—that the writings made by this pen will lead to self-discovery and further growth and evolution."

I spin the pen in my fingers. It is fiery yellow, light, and smooth. Encircling it is the question "Who Are You?"

My heart is full of gratitude for the unearthly power of these tools, which I place inside my suitcase. Curiosa, knowing what this signifies and eager to begin our adventure, tips her head back and lets out a passionate howl.

"Yes," I answer her, as together we gaze in anticipation toward the Earth Realm. "The time for our journey will soon be here."

## CHAPTER 27

### *Soaking in Knowledge*

ONE EVENING AFTER YOGA CLASS I ASKED CURIOSA, "What do we have to lose by going all in with yoga, embracing the philosophies, the lifestyle, the breathing practices, the meditations, everything?"

She barked her assent.

"So what if we lose a few outdated belief systems! My mind could use a good purge!"

She howled in agreement.

"Rules be damned! Good riddance to believe like a child! We're seeking the Great Truth now! Wait, where did the phrase 'the Great Truth' come from, Curiosa? Those aren't my words, and yet they're perfect."

She poked her nose into my chest.

"Wow, a search for the Great Truth!" I exclaimed, rubbing her head and kissing her wet nose. "Oh, my seeking partner, only you know how many years I've longed to trust some ultimate truth. Only you know how I envy people in church who have confidence in the words they read and repeat. Only you know what it would mean for me to find something in which I can wholeheartedly immerse myself, even become a spokesperson for. Yoga must be that path, Curiosa. It feels so right. I don't feel like I'm learning things in Maryann's classes; often I feel like I'm remembering them, as if I've heard them before. Does that make sense?"

Curiosa barked repeatedly as if to underscore my observations.

"If only it hadn't taken me so long to get started. Why, we could have already had eternal joy, maybe even enlightenment!" I complained.

My wolf suddenly sat down and cocked her head.

"What's wrong? You're good with joy but not enlightenment?"

She whined, pawing at the floor.

I sighed, knelt beside her, and explained, "From what I've read in some of my yoga books, enlightenment is the way to joy, freeing us from the pains and frustrations of living in a human body on this complicated planet where only rejection and disappointment await. Enlightenment, Curiosa, will lead us to the truth! It will lighten my footsteps, sweeten my voice, soften my gaze. We can rise above the injustice in the world and focus solely on the bliss from another world. Enlightenment must be the way to joy. Imagine the kind of wife and mother I could be if I were enlightened—calm, peaceful, and loving, with an abundance of patience instead of my quick fuse. I can't go on this way, as you know. Depression waves his cloak at me every single day."

As if to show that while she might have concerns about my motivations she wasn't against the idea entirely, Curiosa grabbed a corner of my rolled-up yoga mat with her teeth, unrolled it by walking backward, then played on the mat in Downward Facing Dog Pose.

I believed with a goal in sight I was finally back in control of my own destiny. And while I might be coming from behind, like when running, I knew how to push myself to the front of the pack. The sooner I could get to the finish line, the sooner I could be the calm, easygoing, type B person I was sure I was.

After about six months of yoga classes with Maryann, I joined every style and level of yoga classes I could find around Minnesota. I ordered yoga blocks, D-ring straps, wool blankets, and trendy yoga clothing online. When my large order of books on yoga and spirituality arrived on my doorstep, I felt as if I'd landed in my own spiritual paradise, where the Tree of Knowledge was bursting with apples ripe for the picking.

In Vinyasa classes, I learned how to move from one pose to the next on the flow of the breath with notable speed, as the teacher guided us in a mixture of English and Sanskrit: "Inhale Warrior 1, exhale Warrior 2. Inhale straighten the front leg, exhale Trikonasana."

In Iyengar classes, I was encouraged to use props to attain proper alignment.

In Ashtanga classes, I repeated the same sequence of challenging poses, with or without props.

In Bikram classes, I did the same twenty-six poses each time in a 105-degree room to sweat out impurities, refraining from drinking water except at designated times.

To maintain my full schedule of yoga classes, I negotiated with my husband: "You go play golf on Saturday afternoons, and then I can take yoga on Monday, Wednesday, and Thursday evenings." On the days my husband was out of town, I'd hire a babysitter and go to yoga. If he was in town, he would come home, I'd give him a quick update on the girls, and I'd go off to nightly New Age class. As a result, between Todd's work schedule, my yoga schedule, and life with toddlers, our marriage began to deteriorate.

Around the house I donned yoga pants and stylish tanks, kicked up into handstands, and dropped into backbends at random. I memorized Sanskrit terminology while pushing my girls on the swings in our backyard and practiced poses in my living room with my television tuned to children's programming. I dreamed that someday the woman pictured on the *Yoga Journal* cover would be me, and inside the magazine would be an interview in which I spoke, with peace radiating from my eyes, about the transformative path of yoga, explaining how my only regret was that I hadn't discovered yoga before having kids so I could have been a better mother.

Though most of the classes I was now taking were more akin to expensive aerobics classes than to the philosophical sessions Maryann had provided, they gave Curiosa plenty to chew on while I picked up new ideas and increased my ability to express myself in the world.

In small ways at first, I tested my reclaimed power. I'd voice my displeasure with the cable company over the phone, or ask for a refill of coffee *after* paying the bill, or give a full-throated "I was next in line" at a chaotic checkout counter. Once I even left an annual holiday party early for no reason other than wanting to go home, slip into flannel pajamas, and read a good book, reminding myself inwardly, "Don't say the babysitter called." And once in a while, in public places I'd laugh out loud with my head thrown back, no hand demurely covering my mouth.

Sometimes people reacted to my new behavior with surprise or respect, some even telling me that it inspired them to speak up for their own needs. Other times people raised eyebrows and clucked tongues in disapproval. Such disapproval was underscored by my own emotions.

"Maybe your voice is getting too loud for society's decorum," Fear would chide.

"What happened to staying small, humble, accommodating?" Guilt would scold, sometimes prompting me to stifle my budding search for truth with apologies.

Watching my voice grow was often like watching a tiny bobber on one of Minnesota's ten thousand lakes: every now and then there was a nibble, an indication of something living beneath the surface that got me excited about the importance of this particular truth. But then Fear and Guilt would slice the line.

❧

My mind continued to be noisy and chaotic during its renovation period. I tore down walls constructed with beliefs about hard work and stoic endurance originating during my North Dakota upbringing. I yanked out the red, white, and blue rug of the American Dream, as well as beliefs I'd held concerning a natural mother's instinct. I removed fallacies of the so-called real world. In their stead, I hung up new curtains—beliefs, themes, and quotes—from the spiritual world and Eastern philosophy. I surrounded myself with sayings about the importance of self-worth, poems about spiritual awakening, and words of wisdom from yogic texts. I tried to undertake my mental renovation the same way I would have a kitchen renovation, but I soon learned that it was not going to be that easy.

If I could give advice to my self of that time, I would explain to her that now, having taken her power and curiosity back, she has a whole lifetime to discard ingrained beliefs and assimilate new knowledge at a realistic pace and to do it slowly, because transforming too quickly can cause instability and confusion, even an identity crisis. But at the time I would have been too hungry to listen to such advice. After all, famine—which for me had taken the form of some authority figure reminding me that spiritual wisdom of this sort, like a dead cat, like Catholic Communion, was never mine to touch—could be just around the corner. My choices, as I perceived them, were binary, as was everything else in my life at the time: feed my hunger or be prey to Depression. I had not yet learned about middle paths.

In fact, "all or nothing girl" was how one of my teachers teasingly referred to me. Unfortunately, my uncompromising mindset resulted in experiencing disappointment when what I needed personally and what yoga asked of me differed. For example, my yoga classes regularly stressed the importance of nonjudgment, which, in the microcosm of the yoga class, meant to not compare our pose or progress with that of others, and in the macrocosm of daily life meant not to compare our inner perceptions of ourselves with the outer presentations of others. I wanted to comply, for I understood the damage—the inability to empathize with oneself or others, for instance—that judgment could induce. But when the teachers said, "Don't judge," I heard: "Don't question, don't challenge; just believe like a child." This time, though, rather than being asked to innocently believe in God I was being asked to blindly believe in yoga. I couldn't do that, because my wolf and I were on the important mission of Operation Great Truth, which required that I question everything in the world, as well as in my own mind, without limitation.

But I couldn't turn back either. Maybe even more than desiring to discover the Great Truth I wanted to belong to the spiritual world in a way I never had to the real world. In my mind, this required becoming a full-fledged yogini—a woman who practices yoga not as a hobby but as a way of life—from my ponytail to my bare feet, from my diet to my lifestyle, from my commitment to practicing poses daily to a commitment to practicing nonjudgment. So I wore ponytails and walked barefoot. I became a vegetarian and practiced poses daily. I perused yoga-related websites and signed up for their newsletters, all in an effort to find my voice, power, and place in the spiritual community I saw as my destiny.

## CHAPTER 28

### Consuming Love

My next yoga teacher, Tara, was so free and fluid in her own body that simply watching her demonstrate poses was a form of meditation. I noted that while Maryann's teachings were like staccato piano—light and quick—Tara's teachings were like the large *djembe* she played—earthy and rhythmic. But, as with Maryann, I sensed her authenticity and instinctively trusted her. While other teachers flaunted big poses and challenged students to lunge deeper and press up higher, Tara modeled how to move slower and feel deeper.

Despite Fear's warnings that Tara was a pagan sorceress disguised in yoga pants and a peace T-shirt, I wanted to experience more of what she offered. So one day I approached her with a mixture of reverence and apprehension and asked if she would take me on as a private student. She beamed. In that moment of choice and trust in intuition, I knew, without yet knowing how, that my search for truth was going to lead me even deeper into the spiritual world.

Once a week for a year I studied yoga with Tara at her home, including yoga philosophies, great yogic texts, and teachings of the great masters. When we practiced asanas, yoga postures, we took time to investigate, feel, yield. Twenty minutes with Tara—breathing, moving an inch at a time, breathing more—was a slow, gentle panacea for my body that had rarely known such care, acceptance, and compassion. With her, life became kinder and more expansive. In the safety she provided, I unraveled more layers of crusty mummy wrappings that had kept my voice and movement in the world stiff, muted, and careful. I confronted and spat out my deepest feelings, beliefs, doubts, and ideas. No matter how often I cringed at my humanness, admitted my shortcomings, or counted my many mistakes, she never mocked or criticized me. As if I had been flying high in my own personal hot-air balloon of perfectionism and denial, she brought me down, one dart of compassion at a time, so my feet touched the earth for a moment and I felt whole.

The only time Tara became annoyed with me was when I held myself to a higher standard than I held others, belittled my own value, or became immersed in my narcissistic ego. Tara's discernment was as sharp as a knife, and she would slice untruths right out of me and invite me to look closer, suddenly making the lies apparent. And then, once the hard work was done, we'd laugh about our collective human condition, at how comfortable we got justifying ourselves as victims or as outsiders. For the first time in my life, I wondered if the true teaching of Christianity was not that human beings should become meek and unquestioning followers in the name of love but that they should find the courage to tame their own inner demons through acts of love, and whether such teachings had not become distorted over years of translation and interpretation.

At any rate, I saw that Tara perfectly modeled what being nonjudgmental looked like in action—not being blind, ignorant, passive, or dismissive but acknowledging everything without expectation, attachment, or aversion. I realized that being nonjudgmental meant to believe like a child, in the way I had first thought—challenging or questioning the very things that often go unchallenged and unquestioned. Ultimately, I made my peace with the teaching of nonjudgment, though today I use the term "discernment" instead, which connotes a gentler, more mindful approach to sorting through thoughts and beliefs.

As part of our year together, Tara also assigned me homework. Sometimes it was a book to read, or a breathing practice to explore, or a mantra to try. But once she assigned me the hardest homework of my life: to look in the mirror and repeat, "I love you." If I couldn't say it out loud, I was to whisper it. Up to this point, whenever I had looked in the mirror I had noticed my too-small breasts, boyish hips, or acne that had never completely disappeared. And now I'd also just cut my hair short, despite my hairstylist's warning that with short hair there would be nowhere to hide.

After Tara had first given me the assignment to look at myself in the mirror and express love, I walked into the bathroom, slowly looked up, and wondered what to do next since the only times I'd looked at myself in the mirror were when I was doing something like putting on makeup or fixing my hair. Just staring at myself felt weird, so three seconds later I walked out.

However, after some time passed I tried again and noticed bright blue eyes sparkling with wit, a smile that hinted at wisdom waiting to be unearthed, and a woman with the potential to nurture herself and others. I saw all that was soft, yielding, and unconditionally loving about myself and embraced these aspects. And then I laughed with that woman in the mirror, seeing, for just a moment, a light in my eyes that transcended this world.

But along with that light I was also aware of a shadow aspect—how impatient, insecure, defensive, condescending, or judgmental I could be. While I could see the value in Tara's efforts to get me to more fully experience my emotions at that time, I wasn't yet ready to allow them to play any legitimate role in my life. Plus, I still remained at least somewhat in solidarity with Depression, who had taught me that the world was an ugly, unjust place where only pain and rejection await. So if I could not trust the world to be a safe place where I could live in love and peace I could not trust my body to be a safe place to live, either. Would a singular focus on enlightenment through yoga be a way to rise above the fray and connect more to a peaceful spiritual realm? I wondered.

## CHAPTER 29

### *Heeding a Calling*

AFTER I HAD STUDIED YOGA FOR ABOUT A YEAR, one of my teachers suggested I look into teaching it. He told me of a weekend training I could take and offered to let me guest teach at the gym where I was taking his class. Because I'd assumed that there was some magical place in the sky where people went to transform into yoga teachers or that they were chosen at birth, hearing that anyone could become a yoga teacher over a weekend at first felt disappointing. However, after my disappointment faded my fingertips began to tingle and my heart lightened. I remembered that I'd always wanted to choose my own adventure, and I saw teaching yoga as an ideal adventure, uniting my love of yoga with my desire to keep growing and to find my purpose.

I began picturing myself at the front of a classroom, sharing yogic wisdom with confidence and gently guiding students into their safest, most comfortable poses. I aimed to be the kind of teacher I preferred, who was unafraid to rub against the grain of what's popular to maintain authenticity, who encouraged questions and expression of emotions, who didn't say, "Don't judge" but instead suggested, "Stay curious about your mind judging." I couldn't wait for my teacher training.

However, the start of my yoga teacher training was nothing like how I had envisioned it. The weekend training didn't teach me much I hadn't already learned, not only disappointing me but making me angry.

"What the hell kind of lame training is this? This isn't yoga but aerobics! This is physical training, not a spiritual training!" Anger roared.

"Keep your hand down—stay unobtrusive!" advised Fear, when seeing me raise my arm to ask a question.

I blushed and, when the athletic, thirty-something yoga instructor called on me, stammered, "I was just wondering, are we actually certified to teach yoga now?" People turned, causing my heart to race and my face to flush.

"This class certifies you to teach yoga tomorrow if you like," the instructor verified.

I was dumbfounded, and Anger ranted, "But this training is insufficient! It's too shallow. It's not right to send people out into the world teaching this rich tradition with so little training!"

After the weekend class was over, I yielded to a letdown similar to one my daughter Cameron experienced when she, at age thirteen, had asked me to make my "special chicken" for dinner, referring to the way I cooked chicken so that it turned out juicy and flavorful.

"Okay!" I had told her, excited about her interest. "And you can watch so you can learn!"

That evening she had watched as I washed the chicken breasts, placed them in a pan, covered them with water, and added two bouillon cubes, explaining that they had to be a specific brand, then turned the burner on.

"That's it?" she had asked.

"That's it!" I had confirmed.

"Oh, I thought there was more to it," she had replied, walking away.

✦

After the weekend yoga training, I upgraded my studies to something with more flavor and texture: private study with Maryann. Although Maryann was a yoga teacher, in her heart she was a philosopher. It had been the philosophy of yoga, not its exercise benefits, that had sent a younger Maryann globetrotting to learn directly from the best of the best—B. K. S. Iyengar, Angela Farmer, and Beryl Bender, among others— though, in the end, she had formulated her own unique brand of yoga.

Maryann was critical of the direction yoga classes were taking in the West, feeling, and I agreed, that too much emphasis was being placed on the physical benefits and sensory stimuli— the use of lights, music, and scents—rather than on accessing spiritual truths through silence and stillness. Yoga, she always reminded her students, is about one thing only: growing more conscious, explaining: "Being conscious, which involves trying to find the meaning of existence, is an arduous path. It costs a lot because it's worth a lot."

From today's perspective, I realize I was given a great gift in having the opportunity to study with a woman who lived her life as she taught her classes—embracing authenticity and acknowledging the truth of who she was with a zesty blend of lightheartedness, courage, and willingness to accept her dark side. Because of her choice to embody her soul, she inspired me to wonder about embodying mine and brought me closer to communication with my soul by encouraging me to acknowledge and respect my emotions.

Between Maryann's philosophical influence and Tara's compassionate one, I probably needed no other teachers. But things were changing fast in the yoga world at this time, and though Maryann had been studying and teaching for decades she had not done the paperwork to sign off on the certificate I would need to teach at most places. So I signed up for the two-hundred-hour Yoga Alliance certified study with a local Minneapolis yoga studio.

Rather than a weekend getaway, this training felt like school. And just like I was back in school I showed up to class on time, turned in all my assignments, and, when asked to give a report with another student, typed up the entire report myself and added her name to the top of the page. But unlike at school I refused to leave Curiosa tied up outside. This meant I raised my hand for clarity as often as I needed to, even if people stared. One fruitful year later I prepared to send ripples of change through the yoga world.

# PART V

## Secretion versus Excretion

❧

*Whether through secretion—*
*moving enzymes, hormones, saliva, and serum*
*through the body to lubricate, protect,*
*and otherwise keep the skin healthy—*
*or excretion—*
*ridding the body of toxic material*
*through sweating or skin diseases such as*
*rashes, acne, eczema, and hives—*
*the body continually promotes*
*greater health and vitality.*

## CHAPTER 30

# Sweet Nectar of Mindful Yoga

My yoga teaching was the sweet nectar resulting from my wild spiritual journey during this period. Initially, I taught yoga in a rental space at a local dance studio and also in a few local churches. Thanks to all my training, I was able to teach students with a variety of skill levels, from beginners to experienced yoginis. I walked around the classroom, occasionally using my body to relay visual cues but primarily relying on vocal instructions to build poses or adjust alignments. Using such themes as balance, effort versus surrender, letting go, discernment, working at the edge, discipline versus ambition, and working from the core helped me maintain consistency throughout classes. I loved and respected my students in a way that I hadn't yet learned to love and respect myself. Like Maryann, I taught my classes with no music, built poses with great attention to alignment, and devoted plenty of time to reflection, silence, and stillness. Like Tara, I taught with gentleness, attention to breath, and compassion for the self.

I named my style of yoga "mindful yoga" and advertised classes in the following manner: "Emphasis on proper alignment and spirituality within the poses. You will learn both Vinyasa yoga (movement with breath) and Hatha yoga (focus on pose alignment). All levels welcome." I chose the term "mindful" both for what it connoted—a deeper, slower, more philosophical approach—and for what it did not—fitness-based classes. To me, practicing mindful yoga meant being present in any given moment to receive its gifts without aversion, attachment, or desire; seeking the deepest truth available in that moment, even if it is difficult to accept; and trusting the wisdom of our bodies instead of just using them. Hence, we began each class with an opening meditation such as the following:

> Imagine that you have brought your best friend's body to class today instead of your own, while she now has yours. You did not exchange rules, you simply trusted that you'd take good care of each other's bodies. As you move through your practice today in your friend's body, notice where the aches and pains lie. Observe the areas of tension and tightness with compassion. Notice also where your friend's body is inviting you to move further inward. Take that step, remembering that once class is over you will return her body to her. She will slip right back into it. You will tell her how much you loved it, how well you cared for it, how beautiful you think it is. She will note how much more expansive and grounded it feels. She will be pleased by how freely her neck and shoulders now roll. She will thank you.

I loved being a yoga teacher. While teaching my classes, I could speak my truth, express my creative power, feel connected to myself and others, and I sensed my innate belonging and duty to the planet. Like the Velveteen Rabbit, I was becoming real; and, in turn, my students were also becoming real. They knew not to expect anything but would show up ready to try whatever their teacher was trying herself that week. As a result, we grew together, becoming a family, and I felt for the first time that, through teaching yoga, I was fulfilling a greater purpose than in any prior pursuit.

## CHAPTER 31

### *Persistence of Anxiety*

"Rasa, do you hear that?" I point up. "It sounds like some-one is shuffling papers in that tree, the one losing its summer leaves prematurely." As I look closer, I spot small, square pieces of yellow paper fluttering in the breeze, and, buried under all the scraps of paper, skittering, yellow eyes. "Oh, that looks like Anxiety. But why is he hiding up in the tree, and why is he covered in all those yellow notes?"

"Those are called Post-it Notes in the Earth Realm. And Anxiety is not hiding in any ordinary tree but the tree of the human body. Do you see how it looks like the human body? The central trunk represents the spine of the body, and the smaller branches and twigs extending outward from the trunk represent the complex network of human nerves."

"And the arms are there, and the legs are there," I add, out-lining the shapes with my hands.

"Exactly. Anxiety is trapped deep inside the nervous system of the human body. The longer he goes unrecognized, the longer lasting the damage to the tree—and to the human body—will be," Rasa explains.

"How do we get him out?" I ask.

"We try to do so through patience and gentleness, because this tree of the human body is at great risk," replies Rasa.

"So that explains why the leaves are falling—Anxiety is draining away the sap of the tree needed for youthfulness and energy," I observe, shocked at the power of this tiny yellow snake to threaten the giant tree.

"Yes," Rasa says, taking my hands in hers. "Make a landing space with your hands, palms up, and invite Anxiety to drop from the tree into your hands. You must be patient. If you think it took a while for Anger to warm up to you, it will likely take Anxiety much longer."

I stand beneath the tree, holding my hands palms up. Minutes pass, then hours as I wait and occasionally see flitting eyes poke out from under the fluttering paper. Finally, the tiny serpent drops into my hands. Seeing that he is shivering, I cup my palms around him to provide warmth.

"Very good," Rasa says, sounding relieved. "Now peel each of those notes from his body to free him before he suffocates beneath all those platitudes."

It overwhelms me to see how deeply Anxiety is buried beneath beliefs. I peel off the first note and read the words written on it: "Don't judge." I observe, "Rasa, this must be from some kind of spiritual community."

"Yes, surely from the yoga community, where the teaching of nonjudgment has often been misinterpreted," she replies, sighing.

"I've read about people who achieve great states of consciousness through the stillness and silence of yoga," I muse.

"I'm afraid you may be in for a bit of a surprise at how things have changed," she comments, laughing.

I peel off the next note and read, "You should already know how to do this."

"Hmm, a holdover from parenting or business, probably. At any rate, that's a good one to shake off," Rasa comments.

I peel off another note that reads, "Setbacks are temporary."

Rasa says knowingly, "That is your ego's husband's mantra. It makes her feel guilty when she doesn't feel better, according to his imaginary timeline."

I peel off the next one, which reads, "Don't let them see you sweat." I ask, "Rasa, what is the problem with sweating? It is detoxifying, is it not?"

"Humans are often embarrassed by the most natural human functions. It is one of their oddest qualities," she explains, chuckling. "However, this note is not about physically sweating but about the idea that no human being who wishes to be successful should show stress, uncertainty, or, for that matter, any uncomfortable emotion, instead maintaining an image of confidence to cover up true emotions for fear that their vulnerability will be seen as weakness."

"All that posturing sounds exhausting," I observe.

"It surely is," she replies. "And, as you know from my guidelines pertaining to the process of soul embodiment, learning to view emotions as teachers and respect them is important to that process. The greatest impediment to soul embodiment is stifling emotions."

"The next note is one I think I remember from when my ego was running. 'Quitters never win, and winners never quit,'" I say, sighing. I stare up at the clear, cloudless sky, thinking if only the mind could be this way, free of platitudes, which, like clouds, pile up, eclipsing the mind until daily life becomes anything but an adventure. I shake my head and observe, "It is a wonder any human can see or feel anything real under all this fake news!"

"Fake news," repeats my soul mate, roaring with laughter. "That phrase sounds familiar, though what it might be used for I cannot say."

I continue to peel off notes until finally all that remains is naked Anxiety, staring up at me nervously. Translucent yellow with rough, dry skin, his movements are shaky and his veiny eyes look as if he has not slept for months.

"Oh, you poor thing," I say as I cup Anxiety in my hands and bring him close to my heart.

"Your instincts about addressing Anxiety warmly are right on the mark. Anxiety requires lots of love, patience, and tenderness," explains Rasa. "And never forget how much love Anxiety also has for you and how distraught it makes him to see you out of balance. This may be one of the reasons he goes to lengths such as we've seen here in an effort to get your undivided attention."

"I will try to remember," I say, not quite able to make that into a promise.

## CHAPTER 32

### *Popped Corn*

ONE EVENING WHEN I ARRIVED HOME FROM YOGA CLASS and began excitedly sharing some new insights my husband said, challenging me, "I thought yoga was supposed to make you more peaceful." The girls were sleeping, and I was talking about philosophical topics while he had been hoping for the kind of connection that didn't need conversation. I couldn't deny that peaceful did not describe what I had been experiencing. Rather, I'd been busily reclaiming over half a lifetime of abandoned or neglected opinions, beliefs, emotions, ideas, hopes, and dreams, which weren't easily exchanged for a sexy negligee. Far from feeling peaceful, I felt like a multilimbed, emotional monster.

"Your husband doesn't like this version of you. He wants a little less talk and a lot more . . . you know," said Shame.

"So these days you're just spending money, not making any?" clucked Guilt.

"I'm still here for you," offered Depression.

Confused and overwhelmed, I went to Maryann for answers about why yoga was not uplifting me to a spiritual and peaceful version of myself but was instead unraveling me. Maryann burst out in joyful laughter and said, "Keri, yoga is not about becoming peaceful. Yoga is about becoming who you are!"

So I'm an oversensitive, unpredictable, impossible-to-satisfy woman? I thought. What if I don't like who I am? What if I want to box up my emotions and return to a state of "ignorance is bliss," not knowing, not asking, and not feeling? Both fearful and awestruck, I wondered if I was like corn once popped, incapable of returning to who I was before.

At this point in my life, bookstores were no longer places in which I found no magic but places where I discovered a little too much magic. One day my eyes were drawn to a colorful cover. I reached out, felt the vibration of something calling from another dimension, and grabbed the book.

"Evil pagan worship, astral travel, and witchcraft? When are you going to stop spiraling further and further away from normal?" Fear admonished.

"But it can't be evil," I argued. "It's just a book!"

"Remember how Eve snuck forbidden fruit in the Garden of Eden? You prove your worthiness to God by walking away from temptation," Guilt urged.

I patted the book back into place.

"We may need your cloak of empty calories soon, Depression!" Fear warned.

"I have the patience of Job," Depression answered.

"Dark magic!" squealed a new emotion.

"Who are you?" I asked this newcomer.

"Anxiety," he answered in a squeaky voice.

"Anxiety, what do you want?" I demanded.

"To keep you away from dangerous things like evil books and dark paths!" he explained.

"Isn't that Fear's job?" I asked.

"Anxiety might be just what is needed to put a stop to all this frenetic searching and get back on God's good side," Guilt answered.

So Anxiety took up residence in my nervous system and, from there, ran up and down my body all day long. Any confrontation with people except for family became increasingly difficult. My body trembled, and I was always cold, the kind of cold that couldn't be relieved with an extra sweater but required a hot bath. Teaching yoga, and ensuring that no one noticed my unsteady body, took immense control. And while Depression's patience may have been endless my own patience with my family and myself was wearing thin.

Yet while my emotions worked together to pull me backward to safer paths, Anxiety could not touch Curiosa, who continued to pull me forward toward greater knowledge. Paralyzed by conflicting forces, I finally acknowledged that it was time for a showdown with my personal equivalent of the dangerous, scaly swamp creature in my adventure books—God.

Discordant aspects of my personality increasingly clashed with each other as I returned again to the church to explore religion. I dressed in a skirt, sweater, nude nylons, and pumps then dropped our toddlers off in the church-provided daycare. But just before I stepped inside the sanctuary my body began to shake and sweat. As everyone filed in around me, I felt like a trapped animal, unable to cross the precipice into the sanctuary. I wanted to scream and run away.

"Get a grip," growled Guilt. "This isn't just about you. You need to give your kids the proper Christian upbringing they deserve, as your parents did for you."

"Yeah, but that hasn't actually worked out so well," I argued.

"Your issues with religion are silly and overblown. Now put them behind you and get inside before you make a scene," Guilt instructed.

I forced my feet forward and searched for my suited-up husband, who'd saved me a place in the middle of a pew. Once I sat down, I crossed my legs, folded my hands on my lap, and tried to pretend that I was comfortable in church. While I sang and repeated words along with the congregation, I fidgeted through the sermon as the pastor spoke of truths I was currently questioning, particularly those that hinted at Christianity being "the only way."

"Don't judge!" said the part of me trained by the yoga community.

"Be good!" the Christian in me retorted.

At home, too, there were signs of my discordant factions. Dog-eared New Age books by Eckhart Tolle, Anodea Judith, Judith Lasater, and B. K. S. Iyengar mingled on my nightstand with books by Christian mystical authors such as St. Teresa of Avila, Thomas Merton, John of the Cross, the anonymous author of *The Cloud of Unknowing*, and the Bible. I wanted them all to be correct, but they contradicted one another. Was there a hell or wasn't there? Did reincarnation happen or not? Did God love us unconditionally, or did a jealous God set strict conditions? Where was the Great Truth I could cling to for the rest of my life? Not just any truth, but the key that could open all life's doors and end all misunderstandings and crises. If only I could sort through all the books, teachers, and wisdom and get to the Great Truth, I thought back then, everything—my relationships, my mind, my life—would settle into a permanently calm and happy state.

But I was at a dead end with books, which did not agree with one another. I was at a stalemate with God, with whom I was not talking. I was roadblocked at yoga class, where I was encouraged to focus only on growing peace and light. I needed my husband to help me break through the tangled mess, but each time I tried to get help from him I rammed into a wall he magically erected anytime something "spiritual" came out of my mouth. Once I accused him of lacking interest in listening to topics about spirituality because he had no desire to grow or challenge himself.

"What happened to the person I married?" my husband retorted.

With tears flowing down my face, my hands in fists, I whispered, "I will never be her again. If you want another bird with a broken wing, you'll have to leave me. If you want me, you'll have to accept me as I am now."

No one was more surprised than I was at the quiet but powerful voice with which I spoke, without my usual desire to buffer my comments with apologies or excuses.

"Okay, let's just calm down," he said, after gauging my seriousness.

Then he explained it wasn't that he didn't care to grow or listen to my concerns but that he was "full up" on religious talk. He said that it took him back to experiences with narcissistic preachers in a high school chapel with their threats of paddle swats and altar antics, memories he didn't want to dredge up.

It finally dawned on me that though our upbringing was very different the result had been the same: neither of us had had the opportunity to explore and investigate spirituality, God, or the meaning of life on our own terms. I accepted his explanation but still expected his help. "I don't know which way to turn. I need help. My problems matter. I can't just make them disappear," I explained.

"Setbacks are temporary," he said softly, shaking his head as if arguing with himself. "You'll pull out of this."

"I don't think so," I answered.

We ended our argument with an agreement: he promised to stay engaged in philosophical conversations as long as he could, but when he felt overloaded or triggered he would say, "I'm full." I, in turn, promised to bookmark my thoughts at that point, as well as make more of an attempt to connect with him in ways that didn't require conversation. Having this agreement was likely a mature decision, given our disparate personal needs and our mutual wish to stay married, but the agreement heavily favored my husband. He never had to step into discomfort, and I never got to step out of it. Going forward, all he had to do was say, "I'm full," and I fell dutifully back in line, which watered down our marriage like from whole to skim milk. Now he wasn't the only one asking, "What happened to the person I married?"

Recognizing the shortcomings of the man behind the calm facade I'd known for seven years was a letdown worse than my first underwhelming yoga teacher training. Judging from the risk he took by showing me his vulnerable side and my disappointed reaction, it's easy to understand why people hide their vulnerability. Because while I wanted to see him vulnerable and told him so, it also frightened me, making me lose my belief that my husband could always be the strong, confident one who didn't struggle or doubt. Early in our marriage I had called Todd a brick wall because nothing seemed to daunt him. He believed that we would always bounce back from difficulties and that setbacks were only temporary. But after the months we lived with colicky babies, my physical and mental health issues, and my complaints about lack of communication and diverging lives, I think we both knew these labels and ideas weren't entirely true.

Indeed, now I was fully popped corn, and I couldn't put myself back into a bag as kernels—nor did I want to. If my husband had left me, I would have accepted that it had to happen that way. I'm not suggesting I wanted to become a divorcée and single mother with no visible means of returning to the corporate work world and with no livable income of my own. I just knew a truth: if I didn't set myself free to search and ponder, apart from Fear and Guilt, I would slowly die inside. There was only one way to the freedom I sought—to move forward.

## CHAPTER 33

### *Map of Opportunities*

A SUDDEN VIBRATION BENEATH MY FEET, reminding me of an Earth Realm earthquake I experienced a lifetime ago, compels all my emotions to come together in bodily form at the precipice. Not surprisingly, a commotion erupts.

"She can't go in there!" Anxiety yells.

"She doesn't have the strength, anyway," agrees Depression.

"She should've already gone in by now," Guilt huffs.

"She should just force her way through it!" grunts Anger.

"Your emotions are arguing over something," Rasa says. "Let's find out what it is."

It is not unusual for my emotions to argue with one another, for while they often desire the same things—safety, respect, to be liked—and while they all subscribe to the philosophy of playing small, except Anger, they use different methods. They generally avoid ganging up on one of their own, unless it's Anger. Yet this time my emotions appear to be spewing venom toward a common enemy in their midst.

We tiptoe closer then disperse the raucous emotion. We pacify Anger, murmur consolations to Anxiety, unburden Depression of its sense of duty, mollify Fear, and address Guilt and Shame. Each emotion serpentines away from the scene to let us souls handle the problem.

In the center, there is nothing but a crumpled piece of parchment paper. Rasa picks it up, smooths it out, and holds it down with four black obsidian stones pulled from her tote bag. "Ah, your map of opportunities has finally arrived. What exquisite timing!"

I gaze at the map, with its fancy scroll reading, "Serene Voyager's Map of Opportunities." In many ways, it resembles an ordinary Earth Realm map, with multilane freeways, dead ends, roundabouts, bodies of water, and rest areas. But it also details my trip's hidden tunnels, secret bridges, unexpected roadblocks, emergency sanctuaries, and, my favorite, brush-covered, full-moon-lit hermit trails. Also unlike an Earth Realm map, which becomes outdated as the world changes, my map can be altered in accordance with the latest choices and circumstances. I practice changing it, my finger working like a magnetic wand shifting the shapes. I pull downward to create a trail around a swamp rather than through it, even though this will increase the distance. I open up a tangled forest to reveal a path inlaid with the glimmering stones of ancient wisdom.

"It's miraculous!" I exclaim. "I have never seen so many possibilities for just one lifetime."

"Each soul has countless options available, all of which are easier to view from this perspective. The Earth Realm, with its rules and unspoken norms, tends to obscure many options. Shall we see where your ego is now?" says Rasa.

"Yes," I agree, "perhaps then we can better understand why my emotions are stirred up."

"Here we are," says Rasa, tapping a point in the center of the map with a red-tipped nail. "She stands before the Tunnel of Authenticity. Oh, my dear, you have led her quite far on her truth-seeking journey!"

Curious to see how she has made her way to this transformative point, I trace my ego's steps backward. I see how she's walked along yoga way, climbed up the branches of the philosophical tree, fought her way through the forest of disbelief, and swum through the oasis of meditation. What a journey, I observe, impressed. But with the Tunnel of Authenticity before her it looks like she now faces her greatest challenges— so it's no wonder my emotions are on high alert. I see that, according to the map, the Tunnel of Authenticity is six to nine months long, yet only wide enough for one human being. Thus it represents an arduous path through a rocky, narrow, damp, dark space with no distance markers inside to let her know how much farther she must travel to reach the end. And yet from here it is easy to see how great the rewards can be for traversing it, for just on the other side lies a life of truth and authenticity, a life of communion between soul and ego.

"Sëri, if your emotions are any indication your ego is uncertain and frightened. It is up to you to encourage her to enter the tunnel, for there are other routes available," advises Rasa.

"Will she be able to hear me if I speak with her using not signs or hints but Earth Realm language?"

"Surely so. The veil between the soul and the ego is as thin as a Post-it Note at the Tunnel of Authenticity. That does not mean she will listen to you, however," warns Rasa.

"Because of her free will?" I ask.

"Yes. Entering the Tunnel of Authenticity is never a requirement as several paths bypass this tunnel. First, there is the bypass of bliss and light, on which the ego simply paints on a permanent smile as if she has found what she was looking for, never revealing the emptiness she still feels inside," explains Rasa.

"That's a painful choice," I observe.

"Painful but common," Rasa replies, honestly. "Second, there is the bypass of bitterness and isolation, on which the ego discounts all progress and lives a quiet, invisible life, a lonely path that inevitably leads to self-hatred and disease." Seeing the shock on my face, Rasa quickly adds, "Don't worry. Your ego has far too much fire to walk this bypass for long."

"That is good to hear," I say, relieved.

"But the same fire that wouldn't allow her to choose the bypass of bitterness and isolation could motivate her to choose the third bypass, the bypass of blame and suspicion, on which she can blame her disappointment and disillusionment on teachers and healers who have helped her, seeing her recent rawness as weakness," explains Rasa.

"Weakness? I see only beautiful vulnerability," I reply.

"Well, often vulnerability is equated with weakness," Rasa says, "and the bypass of blame and suspicion is the most common bypass."

"And yet," I observe, "as divergent as these bypasses may seem they all eventually lead back to the mouth of the Tunnel of Authenticity."

"Yes, but the tunnel grows longer, darker, and more treacherous after each bypass taken," explains Rasa.

"Then it is better to enter the Tunnel of Authenticity sooner rather than later," I conclude. "And what is this here?" I ask, pointing to a large red button next to the tunnel.

"That button opens the door to the tunnel. Only your ego can push it," explains Rasa.

"I will speak to her about that, if she permits me an audience. One final question: Are all the bypasses only temporary, or are some permanent?" I ask.

"Why, there is always this one," Rasa says, pointing to a blinking exit sign placed atop the tunnel's mouth. Hearing my sharp intake of breath, my soul friend replies calmly, "Human life is filled with choices, my dear. So life itself must be a choice, too."

## CHAPTER 34

### *Detox*

As I drove home late one night, heat exploded above my left eye. I prayed it wasn't hives. After arriving home and looking in the bathroom mirror, I prayed again, hoping fiercely that the hives around my eye were only a localized fluke. But by the next morning hives had hijacked my entire body, with the itching excruciating, reminding me of how a friend who recently had had hives described it: "like rolling in a bed of poison ivy." When I have hives, though my skin is hot to the touch I am usually chilly, a hopeless problem since bundling up only exacerbates the hives. The burning and itching originate from within, and if I scratch, histamines are released throughout my bloodstream, making me almost delirious with both temporary relief and knowing that the pain will return with ferocity thirty seconds later.

With previous episodes of hives, I'd seen no other option but to have a familiar unsatisfactory conversation with a doctor, who attempted to help while I held back angry, sarcastic thoughts.

"Have you tried over-the-counter antihistamines?"

"Yes, they don't help." (I may as well be taking baby aspirin.)

"This condition is self-limiting, you know."

"I know." (Does it look like it's limiting itself?)

"Do you think you might be stressed?"

"Probably a little." (What the fuck do you think?)

Finally, I would ask for the only thing I knew that worked: a prescription for Prednisone.

This time, though, I believed I was more educated and could make my own decisions about my health, without relying on doctors or drugs. To motivate myself, I imagined later writing an enlightening issue of my monthly newsletter, entitled *How I Healed My Hives through Natural Medicine and Yoga.*

To self-treat my hives, I first attempted to cool down the surface of my skin using aloe vera, cucumbers, ice packs, the coldest showers I could stand, oatmeal baths, and breathing techniques each day. Then I turned my attention to my nervous system instability. I consulted Doctor Internet and learned such instability could be caused by a vitamin B12 deficiency. I had recently switched to a vegetarian diet, which can, according to Nurse Yahoo, lead to such a deficiency. So I washed a vitamin B12 supplement down with a pot of green tea as a pre-celebration of victory and went to bed.

For hours, my body jolted and twitched. I felt disoriented. My ears buzzed and rang. The internal pressure inside my head was frightening. I dreamt that someone had placed headphones over my ears, turned them on high, and electrocuted me. In the early morning hours, rather than becoming fully awake I remained trapped between realities. I felt as if someone had tipped my bed and I was sliding down slippery silk sheets into an abyss. I woke up thrashing inside wet cotton sheets.

With each passing week, I grew weaker and shakier. Emotionally, I was quick to anger or cry. Fatigue and loss of muscle coordination made yoga practice challenging and teaching it an exercise in self-control.

"She must be doing something wrong. Is she eating an inordinate amount of shellfish? Has she tried scent-free detergents? Ionized water? Taste-free food? A life-free life?" Guilt suggested, checking things off his list as he spoke.

"Nothing works!" Anger roared.

"Okay then, Anger, what do you suggest?" asked Fear.

"Fight fire with fire! I say we burn the motherfucking hives out!" Anger suggested.

"Great idea, Anger. Let's do it," I replied, believing that a good old-fashioned detox was what I needed.

Consequently, I ran the hottest water possible in the tub and poured in a full pound of Epsom salts, which gave off a smoky cloud. I dimmed the lights, stripped off my clothing, and slipped inch by inch into the hot water. Very quickly the pain from the heat blocked the pain from the hives, as if my brain could only process one kind of pain at a time. In a moment of epiphany, I felt compassion for the countless people who hurt themselves in controllable ways to distract from pain that is uncontrollable. My head thumped, my heart raced, and my face dripped with sweat. My hands cramped into Edward Scissorhand–like positions. My lips and cheeks swelled, feeling like small balloons. I didn't know that what was happening to my hands was called tetany, or that the swelling in my face was known as angioedema. I just assumed that, unable to wreak any more havoc on the surface of my skin, whatever toxin was behind the hives had moved inward to affect deeper tissues like my muscles and mucous membranes. Anger's "fight fire with fire" advice suddenly didn't seem so brilliant.

I knew I had to get out of the water quickly, but I couldn't grasp the tub's slippery edge with my stiff hands. I shouted to my husband for help, making nearly inaudible sounds with my swelled lips. After racing to my side, he saw my frozen hands; my red, sweaty face; my puffy lips; my eyes wide with fear. He grasped me under my arms and pulled me out of the tub, then wrapped me in a thick towel and helped me to bed. He massaged my hands until they returned to normal, the swelling in my lips went down, and, finally, the sweating stopped.

My husband asked me if I was okay. I nodded, and he left the bedroom. Unable to reach out to my husband behind my wall of pain and stubbornness, and him unable to reach out to me behind his wall of hurt and feelings of inadequacy, I curled my red, welted body into a fetal position and sobbed.

⮁

A few days later in the emergency room, as a strong dose of Prednisone and Benadryl dripped into my left arm, the hives were forced to retreat, and tears of relief streamed down my cheeks. The emergency room nurse had asked the same types of routine questions doctors had always asked. I answered as I always had: "No, this is not an allergic reaction; I did not change my laundry detergent; yes, I've experienced some stress; I've tried everything you can imagine." And a few things you can't, I thought.

"Do they itch?" she had asked, staring down at an intake form, before admitting me. I glared at her in silence until she raised her eyes to mine and confirmed, "They itch."

Lying in a hospital bed at 3:00 a.m. I cried because of relief from pain but even more due to sadness, overwhelmed by the realization that my life was not as I had expected; my marriage was failing; and my spiritual quest was stalled despite all the yoga and books. Suddenly, I felt dizzy. The room grew darker. I saw odd shapes and patterns moving behind my eyes. My disembodied hand moved toward the call button, but then I let it drop. I felt more alone than I ever had. I wondered who would miss me if I were gone, who still cared about me. My students were home sleeping. My children were home sleeping. My husband was home sleeping while staying with the kids, and even if he could've come we were barricaded from each other in a way that neither of us had the tools to address.

But then I heard a quiet voice from within say:

> *"There are periods in a human life when you feel control slipping away. Everything you have used to support yourself—beliefs, promises, affirmations— dissolve, leaving you with nothing to give you shape.*

*This is part of the process of transformation.*
*For transformation requires melting away all of who*
*you are not, so you can make room for me.*
*I am the me you feel behind your thoughts, the me you*
*touch in the emptiness of your breath, the me you know*
*in the deepest place of your heart. I am your soul."*

I was skeptical of the inner voice being that of my soul. I figured that if I was going to finally meet my soul, the part of me I'd been wanting to meet ever since I first put my body in Legs up the Wall Pose in Maryann's basement, the part of me that lived behind my thoughts, emotions, and breath, it would've been during yoga practice or meditation, the times when I'd listened for my soul so intently I could hear my heart beating—and it would've been accompanied by lights, beautiful images, and angels singing. Surely my soul would not show up for the first time in a sterile emergency room in the middle of the night. But then I heard the voice say:

*"You say enlightenment would free you from the daily*
*pains and frustrations of living, a ticket to a life not so*
*depressing, complicated, and unfair.*
*I say life is adventurous and mysterious, and embracing*
*it wholly is the challenge with the greatest rewards.*
*You believe the Earth Realm is an ugly, unjust place*
*where only pain and rejection await.*
*But I say if we move on together,*

*with Curiosa by our side,*
*we will experience the beauty and joy*
*of the Earth Realm, too.*
*You keep reaching for enlightenment.*
*I keep asking for embodiment.*
*This is what I want.*
*What is it that you want?"*

Pondering that important question, I decided that what I wanted couldn't be that much different from what every human being wanted: to feel authentic; to feel like I belonged; to feel comfort, peace, and love; to be free to be myself; to lead a purposeful life.

After reflecting on my answer to the question, I heard the voice respond:

*"I am pleased to tell you that you are at a crossroads*
*where you can achieve what you long for.*
*Through all your efforts and desires, you have made*
*your way to the mouth of the Tunnel of Authenticity.*
*If you enter the tunnel, a truer path will reveal itself,*
*leading, after emergence, to a more authentic life.*
*But if you bypass this tunnel now,*
*your life will dissolve into a masquerade of*
*emotions and unfulfilled hopes and desires.*
*You must make a choice.*
*An exit and bypasses are as clearly marked as*

*the red button that opens the entrance to the tunnel.*
*You can push away your life and the world*
*without judgment.*
*Life, as always, is a choice.*
*Life is what I want.*
*Wholeness is what I offer.*
*What is it that you want?"*

After hearing these insights about life and death, I realized this indeed was my soul speaking to me, as if the veil between us had thinned and all my work had not been for naught. The thought of being able to hear insights from my soul and respond inwardly was thrilling.

In answer to my soul's question: Yes, I too wanted life, not a life of hurting myself or following ambition in the hope that it would bring me satisfaction. I wanted a life of communication with my soul, from my heart. Suddenly, I decided unequivocally I would enter the Tunnel of Authenticity and do the work required to proceed to the other side, where I hoped a more authentic life awaited me. I pushed the red button.

A moment later a nurse whipped the curtain open, clucked at my pale face, tilted the bed up, took my blood pressure, then left, satisfied that there had been no emergency. I felt myself descend back down onto the bed. I felt blood pulse through my body again. Then I cried for the woman who had been so desperate, so hard on herself. I also cried for the challenging life changes I knew I had to implement to make it through the Tunnel of Authenticity.

✧

Though I had begun to hear the voice of my soul, I did not yet know how to sustain a dialogue with it, so after being discharged from the hospital I reached out to a recommended spiritual guide named Pam, a Franciscan Sister, for help. I told her about my past relationship with Christianity, how I longed to read stories about the gods and goddesses of other religions in such books as the Ramayana or the Bhagavad Gita, and how yoga had introduced me to several more faces of God—many feminine—that intrigued me. Finally, I confided that I felt ashamed of and frightened by my interest, and wondered why I couldn't be content with the religion I was given.

"Gods and goddesses of various religions are merely archetypes of the unknowable Divine," Pam said. "Archetypes are a way to know the unknowable."

"But doesn't it offend God to have images of, or chant to, gods of different religions?" I asked, as I considered a picture of Kali that I had from my yoga studies and ached to hang on my wall.

"You cannot offend God!" she declared. "God is All That Is. How can a single human being offend All That Is?"

"I don't know," I answered, thinking that it did sound outlandish for a human being to have that kind of power.

"If reading the stories of gods and goddesses of various religions appeals to you, explore them," she stated, shrugging in a way that I interpreted not as indifference to the seriousness of my situation but as relinquishment of the power I was trying to give her over my decision. This wasn't the first time someone had tried to hand me back the power I so easily and habitually abdicated, but it was the first time I claimed it. My pursuit of authenticity now demanded I attain authority over my life, deciding for myself what path I was going to take, and my mind was the only place where decisions like this could be made.

Then and there in the courtroom of my mind, a trial took place.

## PLAINTIFF'S STATEMENT

The spiritual seeker inside me desired to dive further into the mystical. Nothing frightened her except stagnation. The unknowns of the universe, the seen and the unseen aspects of the world all intrigued her. She wanted to dispense with time and space and lose herself in the beauty of drumming, chanting, ecstatic dancing, and ancient rituals. She wished to turn away from a judgmental, divisive God and toward a loving, accepting—maybe even feminine—divinity. She didn't want to wait for permission or an occasion to express herself or enjoy her life. She longed to be free and finally exert the influence I'd long denied her.

## DEFENDANT'S STATEMENT

The Christian within me reminded me how diligently he had worked on my behalf to establish rules, and that he wasn't bad but only wanted me to follow socially acceptable behavior so

I'd fit in. Although this had required suppressing aspects of myself, it was for a good cause. His role was backed by over two thousand years of history and pages rimmed with gold. But he was intertwined with Fear and indebted to Guilt.

## Deliberations

If the Christian God told us he loved us but also kept us perpetually frightened, needed to be constantly appeased, always kept tabs on us, and was jealous, then I didn't want a relationship with him. If there was another type of God, one with a more feminine, compassionate, inclusive, nonjudgmental face, then I wanted to get to know her better. The wise words of my first teacher Maryann now made perfect sense: "You'll never get to spirituality through religion." The difference between what I experienced with religion and what I felt inside the spiritual realm yoga opened was the difference between enjoying the smell and sight of ripe pomegranate seeds still neatly in their shell and scooping out the seeds with my fingers, pressing my teeth on them to squirt out their flavor, and letting the red juice dribble down my chin.

## Verdict

I decided, once and for all, that Christianity was not the religion for me. Daringly I added that perhaps no single religion was right for me, and, after a few watchful moments and no negative consequences from the heavens, I settled more deeply into the truth of my verdict.

APPEAL

"Um, Keri? What about me?" asked Guilt, knowing he was an emotion that came along with Christianity.

Unmoved by his sad face, I asked, "What role do you still play in my life? I'm not going to listen to talk about unforgivable sins and fiery hell anymore, you understand that."

"I understand, but there's a lot more I can do for you," pleaded Guilt.

"Like what?" I asked.

"Like this." Guilt cleared his throat and said, "You haven't called your mother in over a week. When's the last time you brought your daughters to the park to swing? Did you remember to send a birthday message to your friend?"

"Okay, Guilt, I'll make you a deal. You help me remember what's important in my life, and I'll let you come along. But you must keep Shame's interference to a minimum. Right now his influence only hampers my growth," I replied.

"I can do that, Keri," Guilt promised, wiping his brow, giving me a crooked smile, and slithering along beside me—no longer a stranger or enemy yet not quite a friend.

One day in February I felt nauseated. I hadn't had my period since Christmastime, but knowing I was not physically pregnant I didn't reach out to a gynecologist but to Pam for an energetic healing session during which I birthed into the world a stronger, more empowered version of myself. As soon as my head touched the pillow on her massage table, I felt the shakiness and emptiness at my core that was the telltale sign of Anxiety's presence. I could've forced my body to stop feeling, as I had done many times in my life, but Pam encouraged me to instead feel my Anxiety without being frightened or disgusted. Soon I was spasming, cramping, sweating, and moaning. I worried that I was sweating right through the layers of sheets to the table beneath. But Pam encouraged me to "keep feeling; keep letting your body speak; you are safe to do or say anything you need" while gently placing her hands on each of my seven chakras, or spiritual energy centers, assuring me that nothing my body did or I said would be judged.

Eventually, the sweating diminished naturally and finally stopped. Then I began to shiver. Pam covered me in weighty blankets. I felt good, aware and cleansed in some way, like I'd been washed, wrung out, and was now hanging to dry in a breeze.

Afterward I struggled to find the words to thank Pam for what she had done for me. I thought she must be part sorceress; however, mysteriously her healing work turned out not to be about casting magic spells but about holding loving space for my body to embody more of its soul. Inside my new, stronger body, I felt my soul slip past the boundaries of self-sufficiency and stubborn independence I'd erected and down into my feet and legs, helping me feel more grounded. I felt her slip into my arms and hands, encouraging me to reach out to others first rather than waiting for an invitation. And I heard her speaking words of deep truth and unflinching honesty. But too soon my soul embodiment process reached a blockade of old pain. I wanted to try to get around it, but my soul told me that after entering the Tunnel of Authenticity there were no more bypasses and the only way forward was to go through it.

## CHAPTER 35

## *Purge*

ONE DAY IN MY THERAPIST'S OFFICE seemingly out of the blue she asked, "Keri, have you ever been raped?"

I blanched. Having had many sessions with this therapist, I trusted her and was willing to answer hard questions—but not this one. I wasn't proud of my one-night encounters or my lack of sexual discernment during college yet had always told myself I had not been a victim.

"God no," I blurted out.

"So you've always said yes," she pressed.

I clenched my teeth, pressed my hands to my face, and stammered, "Yeah, well, mostly, not exactly . . . I don't know."

"Keri," she said, leaning forward, "any sexual encounter not agreed to fully is a form of rape. It doesn't have to be a violent encounter like in the movies or leave you with bruises for it to be a violation of your body. Does that make sense?"

"Yeah, I guess so. I haven't thought about it," I said with uncertainty. "But I'm sure I wasn't ever raped," I assured her, slamming closed her line of questioning. But what my mind couldn't quite remember my body definitely felt: revulsion, an elevated heart rate, Guilt and Fear slithering up my spine like a two-headed snake, a visitation by Anxiety and Shame.

"Well," she said, putting her pen and pad down, "think about it more over the weekend, and let's talk next week."

That afternoon I rocked in my rocking chair in a quiet house, the same rocking chair I had sat in when Depression had offered me his cloak of empty calories almost four years earlier. But I had changed. My mantras of protection—"I'm not a victim," "Never have I lost control of a situation," "I've always called the shots"—unraveled. And then my therapist's questions washed over my heart, rounded into my belly, and slipped down into my loins, where the word *rape* landed heavy, cracking like an egg the protective barrier around my second chakra, the energy center associated with passionate, creative, and sensuous living, leaving me vulnerable. Emotions I'd never let myself feel—bitterness, remorse, regret—engulfed me and overturned my safe little fishing boat called *Just Move On*. I rocked and sobbed for the loss of my innocent, hopeful, trusting self, while drowning in memories that I'd forgotten, dismissed, or devalued.

I remembered the practical joker good-guy whose hands had moved so fast down between my legs I couldn't believe what was happening. I remembered asking him to stop several times, but he wouldn't. Before storming from his house and breaking off our relationship the next day, I had heard him whine that he didn't know what he had done wrong and accuse me of overreacting.

I remembered the guy who had asked to use my bathroom upon dropping me off after our first date and that once he was in my apartment I hadn't known how to get rid of him without first giving him what he had really come in to get.

I remembered the sexy musician who had pushed my head down his body at night but wouldn't get up to help me find my shoes in the morning. I hadn't said no exactly but hadn't said yes either, feeling it had been less risky to do what he had expected than to be called a tease, be rejected, or scorned.

Finally, I remembered the popular high school guy I'd dated several years after graduating whose interest in me, a girl he'd probably never even noticed in high school, left me feeling both dumbfounded and special. I recalled how after I had received the offer to move to California we had spent one last night together, during which I had wanted to tell him that I loved him but couldn't say it. The next morning, as he had held me and I cried good-bye, I remained trapped behind a wall of fear that my feelings could never be reciprocated, a belief based on nothing but random high school hierarchies of popularity, resulting in a different kind of betrayal of my truth and desires.

Compared to many women I had been lucky during my dating years, for I had never faced violent demands or angry, drunken fools grabbing at my body. But I saw that coercion, obligation, reward, guilt, mocking, or teasing was all it had taken for me to fall in line. All those years I'd told myself I had been empowered, but that had been a lie. Now there could be no more lies if I was serious about wanting to live an authentic life. My body needed healing, and healing demanded truth.

Suddenly, whether the word *rape* fit or didn't fit mattered less than the truth that I had not always said yes.

When Todd arrived home, anxious to unwind from a long day at work, there was no Stepford wife mask steely enough to cover the pain on my face or help me say, "Everything's fine, honey. How was your day?" We already had a babysitter scheduled and dinner reservations, so we proceeded to a popular restaurant. There, over pasta at a romantically lit corner table, I blurted out, "I was raped." He knew a lot about my sexual history, but I wanted him to hear it all, for just as I wanted my own life to be aligned with truth I also wanted our marriage to be aligned with truth. I wanted him, the man who had once told me on a California gondola that I was worthy and deserving, to understand why my therapy and spiritual seeking were not making me more peaceful but making me more my authentic self.

However, once the word was out of my mouth, it felt like a stretch of the truth, reflected by the blank look on Todd's face. "What?" he said in disbelief.

I waved my hands back and forth like erasers and explained, "It wasn't rape like you're thinking, never a stranger in a dark alley. I learned today in my therapy session that the definition of rape is wider."

"I dunno what to say," he mumbled into his pasta.

I knew what I wanted him to say—that I was worthy, that I never deserved to be treated with anything other than respect and kindness, that he was very sorry. I wanted him to feel shock, sympathy, anger. But he didn't get angry or offer sympathy—though he might have been in shock since he stared down at his plate, refusing eye contact with me, denying, it seemed, the validity of the very truths I needed to accept to grow into more wholeness.

My heart pounded and my hands shook as I revealed intimate details intended to break through his impenetrable wall.

"Excuse me, could we get our bill and to-go boxes, please?" Todd interrupted, motioning to the server.

He hadn't even bothered to say, "I'm full," but I got the message: he seemed beyond full and likely wondering what kind of woman he had married, a woman with loose morals who had hid her slutty ways. I followed him to the car like a naughty child. If he had called a divorce attorney right there in the parking lot, I would not have been surprised.

Once in the car, I realized that after returning home my chance might be gone to make him listen to me, so I raised my voice as I tried to further explain. But he kept looking straight ahead, with both hands firmly on the wheel.

Then fear kicked my survival instinct into action, and I had an urge to get out and run away. I reached for the door handle, but Todd locked the doors. A voice of reason reminded me that I was ten miles from home and had two kids who needed me. Fleeing was not an option. Fear and Anger wrestled for control of my mind. I grabbed my head in my hands, trying unsuccessfully to stop the spinning, sure I was going to vomit. A traffic light turned red, and, like a woman in labor, I lost control of my body's urges. I twisted toward the door and opened my mouth. I didn't vomit but instead released one long, raw scream. It felt good. The pain diminished a measurable amount. "Do it again," my body begged. This time I clenched my whole body in preparation then screamed as loudly and as long as possible, so I could—

"*Make more room for me,*" said my soul.

—scream out everything I'd always needed to say but didn't know how. I screamed out suppressed self-loathing for not having had the strength to stand up for my body and say no to the men I had dated. Out came the energy ties that still existed between them and me. Then—

"*I slipped further into your body,*" my soul said.

—I screamed out Guilt, an Eve-and-the-snake-and-the-apple Guilt that had no place in who I was. So what if I had been lonely and needy and young. That didn't make me a bad person. There was no more room for judgment or shame. Then—

"*I slipped further into your mind,*" reported my soul.

—I bellowed out rage at those who had preyed on my loneliness, innocence, and trust, and who had never had the consideration to ask for permission, and at a society with beliefs that allowed men to get away with never having to apologize, never having to change, never having to look inward. Then—

"*I slipped further into your heart,*" my soul said.

—I screamed one last time to express that my life experiences, pain, memories, and emotions had value and did not make me silly or weak. I screamed to take up space and speak my truth without apology. I screamed to take my power back.

*"You screamed to live this life with me,"* my soul assured me.

When my purge was over, I collapsed against the car window. Memories of the men receded into insignificance. Free of pain, my body expanded like a genie out of the bottle. I felt light, flowing, almost translucent. My skin tingled. A wildcat's smile played on my lips.

Even while this transformation happened inside my body, Todd's hands stayed on the steering wheel, and he never spoke. At the time, I felt disdain for him and his arrogant, unfeeling male sex. You're full? I thought. Too fucking bad. I am here. I matter. I have thoughts. I have fears. I have emotions. Take me or leave me, but this is who I am. I am body, heart, mind, and soul. Twenty minutes later my old reality descended as our garage door closed behind us.

In my old reality, it didn't matter that the scream had marked the beginning of a new life of greater authenticity. It didn't matter because no one got to act like that and then just go inside a suburban house, set the coffee timer for the next morning, slip into flannel pajamas, and say, "Good night, love." I knew there would be consequences.

Todd went inside the house while I stayed put. He returned a few minutes later and opened my car door. I waited, with my arms up over my face, bracing for the words I was sure would trigger the end of my marriage: "Slut, liar, conniving bitch."

But instead he whispered kindly that he had paid the babysitter and sent her home. He reached his arms out to me. I lowered mine and blinked up at him, still expecting to see judgment, even revulsion, in his eyes. But there was only love and compassion. I crawled into his arms. He carried me into the house and to our bedroom. When he sat me down on the bed, he said, "Keri, I'm so sorry."

The relief I felt in that moment can only be compared to life-and-death matters, like finding out a cancer screening is benign or that a loved one is unharmed after an accident. I poured out to him all the remaining stories I could think of, draining more pain from my body. I was spent but felt amazingly calm and strong. That night my husband never did get angry, threaten to exact revenge, or cry in sympathy. But he listened and never flinched, which blocked Shame and kept the healing process moving.

"Why didn't you say anything at the restaurant or in the car?" I asked him after we'd set the coffee timer for the next morning, slipped into flannel pajamas, and prepared to turn out the light.

"Keri," he said, his hazel eyes filled with relief and love, "I didn't know what to do or say. I just saw you going over the edge. My instinct was to get you home as soon as possible."

&#x2767;

Never since my childhood awakening had I allowed myself to completely let go as I did that night, to scream out anger, sadness, loss, regret until my tears ran dry. I'd only allowed myself to repress emotion, believing it was weak to be emotional and thus allowing Fear, Guilt, and Shame to rule my choices and diminish me so I was a harmless, quiet, careful girl. Even while preparing to bring new life into this world, a feat as miraculous as the birth of a planet, I had worried about offending other people's sensibilities, remaining cautious about making too much noise, shuddering at the thought of doctors—male doctors—hearing me grunt, holler, moan. My body language said, "I don't want to be a bother." I realized that such behavior must come from our collective beliefs about the expected role and purpose of the human body, particularly the female body.

Over the years, I've revisited my experience of the purging scream many times—in my journal, with counselors, with Todd. I've often expressed that I wished my husband could've met me where I was emotionally. But I have come to see that had he tried to feel this on my behalf then I would never have felt it. I would've given myself permission to bypass my feelings, only have named the pain, not felt or released it.

While I don't recommend screaming as a healing modality for everyone, it did help purge me. No tears, no ritual, no journal entry could've so effectively sucked out the black cancer of self-loathing that had grown inside my body ever since Fear and Guilt had made me believe that this is a dangerous world and that outsider girls like me, with too many thoughts and too active an imagination, have to be good and obedient if they want to be accepted. After this purge, I felt like I had emerged from a long, dark tunnel where my vision had been minimal. I had finally chosen to live my life fully on this planet, in this body, with my soul, and with as much authenticity as possible.

## CHAPTER 36

### *Stripped*

THE FULL MOON, JUST VISIBLE FROM the small window inside the sauna, brimmed with new beginnings. I inhaled the earthy, salty scent of dry firewood, old fires, and sweaty bodies. While the walls tried to refuse entry to the winter's howling wind, its fingers slipped in under the door. I pulled my coat tighter around my throat. When I had been at this rural location for a women's retreat a few years ago, the facilitator had pointed out a knotty pine cabin in the middle of the woods, informing the group that the individuals who rented it were referred to as "hermits" and were generally experiencing some kind of inner transformation. I thought those people must be either a little crazy or on to something. Now, having navigated my way to this sauna with a flashlight from that cabin to start a fire, I tried on the label "hermit" as well as the label "crazy," neither of which bothered me. I knew by this time a label was only a label, like one of those name tags people wear at social events and peel off later, and that my essence lay far deeper than any label.

"Everything you need is in here," a woman, looking like she just stepped out of a *Women's Adventure* catalog, had told me when she showed me the sauna.

I nodded, but there were no instructions on its use anywhere, only a matchbook, two tea-light candles burned down almost to their silver bones, an inch-thick stack of yesterday's newspapers, a knee-high pyramid of large logs, and a smattering of branches and twigs. It seemed I wouldn't be starting a fire the way I'd watched my dad do it, given that there were no empty beer cartons, red gasoline cans, or a leaf blower.

I tugged on the metal handle on the fireplace, and the door squeaked open. Inside its belly lay the scorched remnants of many healing fires. I could almost hear the hermits who had come before me join their voices in encouragement, but then my emotions intervened.

"What if you burn yourself? What if you start a forest fire?" Fear questioned.

"Only boys can light fires," Shame opined.

"Why does no one teach these things in school!" hollered Anger.

*"You've birthed babies. You can light a fire,"* encouraged my soul.

I may not have known the proper steps for fire building, but I knew I had the power to light a match and spark my passion back to life. I struck a match several times with no success. Finally, the match ignited with a hiss. Next I lit a tea-light candle and watched its shadow dance around the knots of the sauna's walls. I heard the host of the reality TV show *Survivor* reminding the contestants that "fire represents life."

*"Now, make it bigger and hotter,"* advised my soul.

I crumpled a few pages of newspaper and held them over the tea-light flame, then tossed the flaming paper into the fireplace belly, followed by a few branches, twigs, and leaves. As they crackled and popped, I slipped out of my coat and boots.

*"Now, make it burn stronger,"* urged my soul.

I picked a fat log from the top of the pyramid and placed it onto the fire's beating heart. The room plunged into sudden darkness and silence.

"You are no fire-starter!" Shame lamented.

"See, it's not so easy," Guilt whined.

I had a choice. I could've given up, driven away, and tried to forget about the day I attempted to jump-start my passion. I could've denied that my motto in life was once "Choose your own adventure." I could've gone on to live like a half-conscious zombie, citing as just cause how I tried to be successful in the business world and failed, then tried to become a picture-perfect mother in the parenting world and failed, then tried to enlighten my mind in the spiritual world and failed. Anyone would've understood why I remained safely on the sidelines of life, robotically cheering others on to take a chance on their hopes and dreams without taking more chances myself. But I refused.

*"Too much, too soon, that is all. Take your time.*
*We will learn balance together,"* advised my soul.

I picked up a forked tool and gently lifted the fat log. I found my flame, still burning but cooling down. I held my breath and waited. As I offered my flame space and time, it sucked up fresh oxygen then spread around the log's edges and expanded into a confident, amber glow. I set the log back down with satisfaction.

Within minutes the fire was as lusting as a lover. I raised my arms overhead and bowed in front of the roaring crowd. Even Shame offered a congratulatory wink. I closed the sauna door and clicked off the borrowed light, for I had made my own. "Now what do you think of that?" I said out loud.

"*I think it is magnificent*," my soul replied.

"Wait—you heard that? I thought I was supposed to listen to you, not the other way around. You and I, we can talk like people?" I asked my soul, amazed to discover that soul communication worked both ways.

"*Of course, we can. It is no different from how you communicate with Fear, Guilt, or any other emotion,*" my soul assured me.

"Well, if that's the case, I have some bones to pick with you, starting with why I have such intense emotions," I said.

"*We can do that, Keri. But you just transformed this frigid, dark, lifeless space into a healing sweat lodge. Enjoy it.*"

My soul had advised wisely. I peeled off the rest of my clothing and lay back on the bench, where I let sweat and pain ooze from my body. With the backdrop of the roaring fire, my soul and I burned with a fresh lust for life.

"We're all in this life together now, and, along with Curiosa, we will walk from this fire back into the world," I said to my emotions and my soul, welcoming home these parts of myself I'd so often denied.

My soul pointed out, *"Did you notice that it wasn't*
*a single healing mantra, book of spiritual secrets, or lesson*
*from a master teacher that made you strip and surrender,*
*but rather your own painful and imperfect*
*non-enlightenment-achieving experiences?*
*This insight may be a piece of the Great Truth!"*

"Yes, I do see how my own emotions and life experiences have helped in my transformation. But the books, teachers, and mantras—they have aided me too, haven't they?" I asked, suddenly wondering if all my seeking in outside sources muddied the truth rather than informing it.

*"Most certainly those sources and techniques have helped you!"*
my soul insisted. *"But you see, none of them alone*
*embodies the Great Truth but rather is a piece of a puzzle*
*I have been working on for lifetimes and will,*
*I suspect, for many lifetimes to come.*
*Their purpose, which they served well,*
*was to guide you to remember and embody me."*

"So you were never expecting me to figure it all out," I mused.

I heard my soul chuckle. *"Hardly. Though it is
not surprising that you interpreted my passion this way,
given your orientation to the ambition so common in
the Earth Realm. Rather than a goal to attain,
spiritual seeking is a means through which
a human being can embody their soul.
The more you continue to embody me in moments like this,
the more clearly I can guide you as we continue the search
together,"* she informed me.

"I can still read books, then?" I asked, hopeful.

*"Why, of course!"* my soul stated. *"But now,
you have the Comb of Discernment,
the Mirror of Self-Love, and the Pen of Reflection.
You can use these in tandem with books
and outside knowledge to make better informed decisions
and to keep yourself inspired and grounded."*

Relieved, I let myself feel deeply. I noted a sense of well-being throughout my entire body—my blood pumping, my heart open, my skin tingling. "Embodiment feels good," I said.

*"Indeed,"* agreed my soul.
*"I am so very glad you have chosen this path."*

That night I was sure that if the first part of my search for the Great Truth had been like diving into a long-awaited main course of meat and potatoes, the next segment would feel like indulging in a dessert of raspberry ice cream topped with chocolate sauce and wild huckleberries.

❧

As a result of my personal transformation and more regular conversations with my soul, I changed the way I played the various roles in my life. I changed in my role as a spouse. Together, my husband and I saw a therapist, who guided us through our underlying issues. My complaint about Todd was that I thought he was purposely trying to hold me back from spiritual growth. But what I needed help to see was that though he wasn't equipped to encourage me on my spiritual journey he helped ground and encourage me in other, equally important ways—like getting out into the world to enjoy the simple pleasures of interacting with others. To support my spiritual quest, I had many teachers and healers.

I changed in my role as a mother. My relationship with my children, now five and three, became smoother. Because I was now unafraid of my own emotions, I wasn't afraid of their emotions anymore either. More grounded in my body, I began to better appreciate the role of mother as a true spiritual practice.

I changed my relationship with Anxiety. I had once confided in Tara, my teacher of self-love, that the small group introductions we did in her yoga workshops triggered my anxiety while awaiting my turn. Compassionately, she invited me to sit on her left side at the next workshop and begin the introductions, which gave me a sense of control. This was our pattern for some months until one day she smiled at me, winked, and then began with the person to her right. She knew, as did

I, that while I had not conquered Anxiety I could sit with him more comfortably.

And I changed my role as a teacher. After my emergency room visit, I had typed an email to my yoga students admitting my illness and announcing the temporary cancellation of my yoga classes. I had been afraid that when I was ready to come back my students would've moved on. But they waited for me, and when we started again I was speechless as one of my students said, "I'm so glad you're back. But I didn't think you could get sick!" This made me realize how well I had hidden my pain from even the people who brought me the most joy. From that point on, I opened myself up more, letting people see the real me, and in return I experienced deeper relationships than before. I finally learned what I'd been teaching all along: that vulnerability—the willingness to share all the parts of ourselves that make up who we are, including our discomfort, pain, pleasure, worries, successes, and shortcomings—is a strength, not a weakness.

While I rightly considered my spiritual growth as largely an internal development, I had yet to test my new inner tools and healthier mindset in significant external situations. Had my life been a movie at this time, I thought I'd be at the point where I had just won my first lightsaber match with Yoda, pulled out Excalibur's sword, or just told Nala that I, Simba, would return to the Pride Lands. Yet I was confident I could cope with anything else with which the world could challenge me.

# PART VI

## *Regulation*

❦

*The skin seeks a homogenized environment.*
*Through shivering, sweating,*
*or increased metabolic reactions,*
*it keeps the body's temperature within*
*normal parameters.*

## CHAPTER 37

### *Center of Mindfulness*

ONE DAY I WENT TO A COFFEE SHOP FOR A MEETING WITH Meredith, a woman I had met at a yoga workshop I'd offered at a studio she part owned and to whom I planned to describe the newly envisioned center of mindfulness I hoped to establish. A few weeks earlier she had told me she was experiencing partnership conflicts, while I had told her about my family's upcoming move to a suburb where, coincidentally, she lived.

Though my husband and I had sought to be normalized by moving to a suburb, I, now thirty-five, sought to normalize myself by ceasing to be a nomadic yoga teacher and building a more permanent venue for students and a more professional reputation for myself. When I had met Meredith, a self-assured businesswoman and yoga teacher twenty years my senior, I wondered if we could become partners in building the new center were she to end her current partnership.

Meredith entered the coffee shop in a whirlwind of charisma and confidence. She was tall, of medium build, and with long, graying hair down to her shoulders. Her green eyes, magnified by red librarian-style readers set upon a long, angled nose, were small and sharp. Watching her body language—shoulders back, neck long, chin angled up—and the way she ordered at the counter, I knew that she was accustomed to being in control of her life, free from anyone's power or influence. Her facial features and the way she tilted her head when she listened reminded me of a red cardinal, bright, quick, and watchful.

We began our meeting with small talk, bonding over some common struggles in our roles as wives and mothers. We exchanged respect and admiration then moved onto deeper topics, discovering shared frustrations about prior attempts to fit into established religion. For this reason, we both felt indebted to yoga for helping us find our own path and agreed that for us it was a way of life, calling ourselves yoginis. I revealed personal health issues, such as my recurring hives. I told her how I built my yoga business from scratch, and the joy I took in regularly adding new creative elements. And finally, feeling comfortable about our connection, I shared with her my vision for a center of mindfulness, a place for people serious about their spiritual growth where they could explore various contemplative practices, including yoga, tai chi, qigong, and diverse seated and walking meditation techniques, with mindfulness as the common element. A distinguishing feature supporting this vision would be a cozy gathering space where people could linger, sip tea, and read books provided.

As I talked, Meredith's eyes mirrored back my own enthusiasm, and I hoped she would see the center's potential. I was sure that she was the right partner for the enterprise, with her outgoing personality and confident approach to the world the necessary yang to my yin.

I looked at the two of us through this lens of yin and yang because between the time of my fire ritual in the sauna and the time of this meeting with Meredith I had been teaching yin yoga, a practice that contrasts with many popular styles of yoga due to its softness, stillness, and silence. While yang is associated with the archetypal masculine energy, yin is associated with the archetypal feminine energy. Yang energy is hot, quick, light, and bright, while yin energy is soft, slow, reflective, and receptive. With the yin yoga philosophy guiding us, my students and I moved deeply into our tissues and bones, while more gently probing our minds and hearts.

After what was to me an intimate and revealing conversation, Meredith abruptly departed for another appointment. I sat alone a while longer, trying to dismiss a memory brought to me courtesy of my worrisome companion Fear. During my short tenure working for the company in Los Angeles, my coworkers, supervisors, and I had met to discuss the rollout of a new system. In my opinion, the entire project was being rushed, leaving us primed for problems. So, determined not to make another Great Mistake, I had advised caution and thorough testing. A day later my supervisor's boss, a grandfatherly figure, had requested a meeting with me. When I arrived at his office, he had welcomed me warmly and shown interest in me personally, telling me to let him know if there was anything I needed. Then he had asked me my thoughts on the system rollout, saying he had heard I had some ideas. Though apprehensive about speaking up to this authority figure, I hoped that if I could impress him with my newfound wisdom he would ask me to supervise the project, so I offered my observations. When I finished, he curtly thanked me and sent me out. Walking back to my cubicle, I wanted to keep my head up high, but humiliation won out. After all, it hadn't been a free exchange of ideas—just me giving him a striptease of truth. Later the corporate grapevine buzzed with the news that this man believed me to be both arrogant and out of line. My coworkers advised me to keep a low profile.

Now, after describing my vision of the center of mindfulness to Meredith, I had the same ominous feeling as when I'd offered my ideas in the business world. I reassured myself, while simultaneously sensing something was off.

"She left so abruptly after you shared so intimately," Fear observed.

"She's a businesswoman. She was probably just busy," I replied.

"But is she the right fit to partner with you?" Fear persisted.

"She's the yang to my yin; we're opposite but equal," I insisted. Yet despite the uneasy feelings after my meeting with Meredith, at the time I believed in my vision for the center, Meredith's potentially valuable role in it, and the significance of our serendipitous encounters—with a passion I'd never felt for any religious dogma. Looking back, it was almost as if I believed like a child.

CHAPTER 38

*Seeds of Creation*

AS THE DAY SHIFTS TO EVENING IN THE SOUL REALM, clouds drift into view in the shape of humans gardening peacefully together—planting seeds, watering them, plucking the ripened fruit as necessary so there is no hunger or poverty. There are no poisonous apples, evil snakes, or eternal punishment. This cloud-vision, called Garden of the Shared Purpose, keeps me hopeful as I contemplate some potentially dark times in the Earth Realm.

Fortunately, my packing is nearly complete, although there are still a few remaining items, one of which Curiosa now chases. Rasa and I watch Curiosa track the moving flat, rectangular package wrapped with twine over and under the settee, through the lilies, lotuses, and marigolds bordering the River of Forgetting, and into the pond, finally catching it. She trots back and drops the package proudly at my bare feet.

I pat her head, unravel the twine, tear open the package, and pour out seeds of all shapes, colors, and textures into my open hand. Each seed, having a consciousness of its own, speaks of its dream for manifestation.

"Listen to these seeds of creation!" I exclaim, holding out my hand for Rasa to hear. "They're bursting with ideas to plant in the Earth Realm. Once I'm embodied, I'll plant new ones each day, everywhere I go."

Rasa leads me back to the settee and says, "While in the Soul Realm, it is easy to forget that in the Earth Realm limits exist. You are correct that each of these seeds speaks to a possibility. But no soul could, or is expected to, plant all these in one lifetime. And even if planted many are never intended to become mature plants. For that is not their purpose. As you may recall, human life is not only about birthing and manifesting ideas but about releasing them, too. In the eyes of the universe, these are three equally important acts, each making the next one possible."

"I cannot imagine letting any of these go," I say, looking appreciatively at the seeds in my hand. "They are pure, innocent, and full of potential."

"And some are still immature, too," states Rasa, chuckling as she plucks a tiny, squirming seed from the top of the pile. "Take this one, for instance. It bursts with enthusiasm but is not yet fully developed and so could sprout in a number of unexpected ways, perhaps providing many learning opportunities but also disappointment at not matching your ideal vision."

"Maybe, then, I should leave that one behind," I say, considering the seed. "I could take it another time."

"You could do that, though this seed has some unique

properties. It could play a critical role in your continued search for the Great Truth. If you leave it behind, you may always wonder 'if only,' the phrase human beings use when expressing regrets."

I squint at the tiny seed, able to discern both its potential and its lack of development but decide that if it can further refine my understanding of the Great Truth it is worthwhile to plant. I slip the seed back inside the package and hold the package to my heart.

My soul mate looks toward the sky, where the cloud shapes have merged into an indistinguishable mass of gray, portending rain. She digs inside her tote bag and pulls out yet another bottle of wine and a crystal decanter shaped like a magic lamp. "Rain is coming," she warns, "and by the appearance of the sky it will last for some time, which means we have time to let this red breathe before we drink it."

Then, on the afternoon before my departure, the clouds release a hard but refreshing rain. The branches of the redwood tree that form parts of the settee now twist higher, then weave a roofed gazebo for two contemplative souls, a curious wolf, a decanter filled with red wine, and a package of antsy seeds. We wait with anticipation.

## CHAPTER 39

### *Business Plan*

AT FIRST JUST MEREDITH AND I HAD PLANTED THE SEED of our new center under a summer sky. We had only each other and a tiny planted seed that we nurtured like helicopter parents—until one Saturday morning when Meredith brought a third partner to the venture. Meredith had told me that this day I would meet Stacy, who had expressed interest in getting involved in our center. I had questioned why we needed an additional partner, but Meredith had quickly assured me that a third person would be an asset, and that, as a full-time corporate employee, Stacy wasn't looking to disrupt our process but, as someone with a passion for yoga, only wished to support the center. Stacy seemed to be thoughtful, modest, and likable. Plus, I could see how it might be beneficial to engage a third partner, such as having a tie-breaker for important decisions. So I dismissed the reservations I had regarding Stacy and Meredith's history, about which I knew little. Since we were all yoginis living in the spiritual rather than corporate world and following the Yamas, the first limb of the eight-limbed path of yoga that laid out a code of ethics not unlike the Ten Commandments, I believed we could overcome any disagreements.

The next step in manifesting our vision was to find a suitable location for the center. The three of us spent several weekends searching, ultimately setting our sights on a brand-new development in our neighborhood. As we toured the bare-bones space, I could hear the ding of the meditation bell, taste sweet passion fruit tea, visualize students' winter boots cluttered by the doorway. We all agreed that the space was perfect. We jointly decided to purchase, rather than lease, the property, which made financial sense. Not caring how much we resembled a yogic version of *Twister*, the three of us had dinners with each other's families, toasting our deepening ties.

During this time, a few cautionary voices attempted to interrupt the celebrations. First, my husband suggested, "Keri, do you think you should slow things down just a little?"

"Please," I replied. "I just want to try building something of my own. This opportunity may never come again. I don't ever want to have to wonder 'if only.'"

"I don't want to see you get overwhelmed, that's all. You're already so busy. You just started feeling healthier not long ago. But I'll support you if this is what you want," he declared.

Then my dad warned, "Keri, you haven't known these women very long. Are you sure it's a good idea to be on a thirty-year mortgage with them?"

"It's fine, I trust them," I replied as lightly as I could. But I swallowed my bitterness. My dad's advice sometimes sounded too logical and dismissive of my feelings. For example, once when my oldest daughter was about six months old and I'd received an attractive job offer but struggled with whether to take the job, he had suggested, "Draw up a pro–con list." But after writing the list I had concluded that in potentially life-changing circumstances it was impossible to measure the emotional impact on a two-dimensional sheet of paper.

Still feeling connected to my soul, I longed to take the kind of risk only the bravest visionaries take. No one could stop me, not even myself, when my body cautioned that since I'd committed to attending to the needs of my body I should keep the plan of a center simple and stress-free.

"But we can't listen to such nonsense. We have worth to prove and success to achieve," insisted Fear, raising a glass and toasting. "To being a visionary!"

"To being a visionary," Anxiety mumbled in agreement.

Soon Meredith, Stacy, and I were finalizing our business plan and applying for a loan with the help of a lawyer. "You need to designate a president, a secretary, and a treasurer," our lawyer announced as we sat around a boardroom table one day. I understood the need for legal documents if we hoped to get a loan, but I cringed at the thought of establishing a hierarchy for what I considered an egalitarian venture.

"What does it mean for one of us to be the president on paper when in all other respects we are equal partners?" I asked, feeling like a schoolgirl posing a question when everyone else is itching to go to lunch.

The lawyer answered, "You will be signing formal documents, including checks to your teachers and service providers, so you need formal titles." The lawyer reassured me that our power, voices, and ownership remained equal despite titles. My partners, rather than voicing reassurances or concerns of their own, remained silent.

"I understand," I said, eager to relieve the pressure of three pairs of eyes on me.

I had already volunteered to balance the company checkbook and compile the end-of-month reports, so I was a natural pick for treasurer. It made sense that Stacy was secretary since she was going to be only minimally involved. Meredith then, by default, became the president.

I could've been concerned about how my smile was a bit forced, my handshake a little sweaty. I could've said no or walked away. But I wasn't able to do any of those things because I saw this as my final chance to develop all the things no one had ever given me—purpose, belonging, and joy.

A few weeks later Fear, perhaps regretting not speaking up earlier, said, "Keri, we need to talk."

"What are you worried about? I thought you were on board with the business plan," I replied.

My body, too, had been sending cautionary signals I didn't dare dismiss, like insomnia, nightmares, and a deepening fatigue. I booked a retreat weekend so I could address the fear I sensed building up inside before it exploded into hives, or worse.

❧

Settled in my hermitage, I thought first about my yoga family. Though several members would be joining me at the new center to continue our journey together, others would not be. I was simultaneously sad that our family was being broken up and excited about the future.

Next I reflected more about what Meredith, Stacy, and I had built together. I admitted that we had created a nice yoga center but not the center for mindfulness I had initially envisioned. It was when we had discussed whether or not to offer hot yoga that I had felt the first departure from that vision. I agreed with my partners that some like it hot and competitive (even myself on occasion) but argued that our center was to be built on a shared purpose of mindfulness and community. Since we had decided that to honor the highest purpose of yoga we would leave yoga-booty-ballet, yogalates, and other trendy combinations to more fitness-oriented centers, I had justified the inclusion of hot yoga in our business model as just a tiny addition that could not take away from the whole.

Finally I was ready to address Fear, who admitted, "I'm afraid of failure."

"Me, too. But you have to take chances in life; you have to believe things will turn out okay," I insisted.

"I'm also afraid of judgement and criticism," added Fear.

I replied, "Being an owner will require more strictness and rules, granted. But we've been creating on our own a long time, so we're ready. And if we get criticized, we have tools to handle it, given to me by my soul: the Comb of Discernment, the Mirror of Self-Love, and the Pen of Reflection. The layers between us have grown thin, so I'm sure it'll be easier to communicate with her now and get advice about how to use these tools. Besides, the center of mindfulness was originally her idea," I asserted.

"But to hear her you have to be willing to feel and listen. You can't be too busy to do that," Fear reminded me.

"I'll make time, Fear," I vowed.

"But I'm afraid of losing all the freedom we've gained," Fear admitted. "I used to be afraid of slowing down but not anymore."

"I promise I will watch my energy level. Remember, I'm not in this venture with corporate people but with spiritual people who will support me if I have to take a day off. And we will have access to healers right in our own center. With so many mindful people in the center, the cards are surely stacked in our favor. I know we had to draw up that stupid business plan. Ignore it. Here's my business plan." I drew a heart on a pad of paper, around which I wrote phrases about how I could stay healthy and strong as we began this venture: "Admits mistakes and asks for help; sets boundaries; leads with the heart; listens to soul." Inside the heart I listed the attributes I hoped to embody: "Courage, humility, softness, calmness, approachability, patience, and strength."

Then, reassuring Fear further, I said, "If we remember this business plan, everything will be fine. Do you trust me?"

"Do I have a choice?" Fear replied, reluctantly.

Had I dug deeper at the time, perhaps I could have seen that what I feared more than anything was becoming insignificant—a woman without a clear mission, a title, a classroom, or a platform. But this fear was ingrained so deeply within my being that it would take a future apocalyptic experience to acknowledge and eventually purge it. My soul, always a greater risk-taker than me, closed the discussion with words:

*"Well, then. Bring on the apocalypse."*

## CHAPTER 40

### *Departing Visions*

AFTER HUNDREDS OF DECISIONS MADE JOINTLY about flooring, walls, and lighting, the center was a work of art. When visitors walked in, they first saw a row of cubbies and racks for leaving jackets and shoes. Then they stopped by the front desk, where they checked in for their classes or healing appointments. Behind the front desk were two yoga studios, one with its own thermostat for the hot yoga classes and both with built-in cabinets for blankets, blocks, straps, and extra mats. Downstairs were several private office spaces. At the core of the building was the Gathering Space, a good-size seating area plus a kitchenette where eight to ten people could comfortably gather. To furnish it, I had brought from my house two plush yellow chairs, and Meredith had contributed a coffee table. Along one wall were large windows that looked out over a pond visited by geese. Along another wall I had installed a long, black bookcase and filled it with books for people to check out or read at the site. I had also brought a full-size refrigerator, dishwasher, and microwave oven so students could make tea and snacks, and our teachers and healers could have lunch. We had accessorized the space with more chairs, pictures, and throw pillows. As a result, the Gathering Space gave the impression of being a haven from the pressures of money or status prevalent in the outside world.

Everyone who came through our doors gazed in awe at what we had built and then handed over their credit card to purchase classes, clothing, and gift cards. As we had hoped, practitioners of many alternative modalities—massage, acupuncture, healing touch, aromatherapy—had agreed to lend their services to our vision. The money we charged healers for rent went toward our mortgage payment. By year's end, we had easily met our initial budgetary goals. But by the end of January, as the holidays ebbed and the excitement of something-new-on-the-corner wore off, the cash flow slowed to a steady stream, though we were still in the black, a positive omen for a new business. I hoped these results meant that the business would grow and I could refocus more on self-care. I loved the space we'd built for others but missed the space I'd carved out for myself. I was teaching more classes per week than I ever had before, plus working at the front desk during weekday hours, updating the website, planning workshops, writing newsletters, maintaining the online student tracking system, and taking care of the financial duties required of me as the company's treasurer. Even as I encouraged students and clients to let go of the various skins they wore and reveal their souls, I was layering up my own skins.

One day when Meredith and I had finished assessing the

month's profit and loss statement, she expressed concern, perhaps because business appeared to be leveling off or because we seemed to be settling into a routine. I didn't share her concern at the time because of my faith in my soul's vision, as well as my confidence in the center's early results, the partnership, and the original vision. So I reassured her, saying, "Class attendance is good. Holiday gift cards run out in a few days, and people will pay again. Have faith, we'll be fine." In hindsight, perhaps I didn't fully appreciate the risk our families had taken by guaranteeing the mortgage if the center couldn't make sufficient profit to cover these payments.

Another morning at the center I saw flyers on the doors advertising an upcoming workshop there, depicting a beautiful, young, thin woman smiling down at a measuring tape wrapped around her waist. The image encapsulated all that I hated about what had happened to yoga since it had gone mainstream—the way it was now marketed as a fitness program rather than the ancient spiritual practice it truly was, with an emphasis on the physical over the spiritual, the material over the intangible, instant gratification over slow change. In my mind, I could hear the voice of my teacher Maryann saying, "Yoga should have depth because it's a spiritual philosophy. There's no depth to jumping through poses; you might as well be dancing."

Considering these flyers, which I had not agreed to post, an offense to my vision, I wanted to rip them up. The Meredith I had met in the coffee shop a little over a year before wouldn't have agreed to them either, I thought. That day we had both lamented the commercialization of yoga, its being co-opted for profit while stripped of many of its spiritual aspects. And we had both agreed that our center would take the hard path of authenticity over the easier path of superficiality. I thought I just needed to remind the new business-minded Meredith about the old spiritually leaning Meredith. But it took only seconds for me to realize that I was not approaching the woman with whom I'd shared grand ideas about the center. Not only did this Meredith offer a robust argument for aggressive marketing, but her body language—shoulders turned away, chin lifted, back rigid, eyes anywhere but on mine—told me that she was the president and had sole discretion over decisions such as this.

Consequently, the flyers stayed on the doors in one piece, but the trust between us ripped in two. I acknowledged what I'd sensed but not admitted: Meredith's approach was in direct opposition to mine at every turn. I wanted to plan, test, practice, and then let go and trust; she seemed to create problems then thrive on solving them at the last minute. I was ready to trust the organic growth of a well-planted idea; she was gearing up for a fight.

Over the next summer, we had arguments about almost everything, such as the following:

Me: We agreed that Pilates doesn't belong in our business model, remember?

Her: Keri, you'd see Joseph Pilates was an amazing man if you'd just read his book.

Me: We shouldn't give classes away for free for a month—it will diminish their value.

Her: How else do we get people to try them?

Me: We shouldn't hire a teacher who is only certified to teach one kind of yoga. We want more experienced, well-rounded teachers, remember?

Her: Keri, this person is very nice and a good teacher.

Me: Skin care isn't in our business model.

Her: We need to rent space, Keri.

Between arguments, I constantly felt the need to apologize and explain myself, while she never did, sounding to anyone in earshot, including myself, like the practical, reasonable half of the partnership. I was beginning to understand that I was coming across as an inflexible, elitist yogic snob who didn't understand the sacrifices grown-ups need to make to succeed in business rather than as a devoted yoga teacher who wanted to offer something pure and of the heart.

My emotions also started challenging my relatively new self-image and the viability of my soul's vision:

"You learned long ago that business does not reflect your true self," reminded Shame.

"It's as much a part of who I am as anything else," I countered.

"If it doesn't work out, there are other options," Depression offered.

"I'll make this work somehow," I answered, desperate to avoid future run-ins with Depression.

Little questions rolled into bigger ones, until I soon began to question who I was, how I felt, and what I was fighting for. So when one morning Meredith commented, with exasperation, "Keri, I never know what to expect from you—one day you're easygoing and chatty, the next you're closed off and touchy," I couldn't answer. I was at least as confused as she was.

The center, too, was hopelessly straddled between growing into a haven for reflection and mindfulness and becoming a yoga center/gym offering hot yoga and weight loss tips. These incompatibilities caused equally incompatible reactions among various parts of myself:

"If you were a real yogini, you'd just focus on teaching your own classes in keeping with the vision."

"No, you must speak your truth and fight for the original vision for the entire center."

"You need to be more accommodating. Go with the flow!"

"No, do the 'Minnesota nice' thing. Pretend you're fine. Don't let them know they're getting to you."

Amidst the many contradictions, I could no longer distinguish the voices of my emotions from the voice I needed to hear most—that of my soul. Thus, I began working once again from my ego's ambition rather than my soul's passion.

As spring turned to summer then fall, the gap between my original vision of a center for mindfulness and what we had manifested continually widened. Like when a beautiful, soft sweater you order online arrives crumpled and cheap-looking,

I was disappointed by the optics I'd bought in to. But customer service—the president, in this case—dismissed my complaints with frustrated sighs and ad hoc lessons in Marketing and Business 101.

Picture this as a movie: me starring in the role of an elitist, dogmatic, even fanatic yoga teacher and Meredith starring as Madam Business, standing up for logic, practicality, and all things sensible and safe. Our designated costumes reflect pre-set beliefs, catchphrases, and sound bites, all but eliminating any potential for negotiation. If I was going to play the elitist and stand up for truth, trust, and taking chances, then I needed to hold that line, while Meredith had to make the business work—through micromanaging and analyzing. Both of us felt we had to maintain our respective stances, leading us to increasingly respond with reflexivity rather than courageous examination; with ideological rigidity rather than creativity; with protective justification rather than open curiosity.

Yet despite our sometimes different stances the Gathering Space really did work magic. Between or after classes, Meredith and I would sip tea or wine and share food there, laying down our weapons of words and engaging in conversation at a level of intimacy that few people do. During such times, the smoldering remains of hope within me were rekindled. On nights at home following such encounters, I'd remember the reason I had wanted to create the center and dream of a garden of shared purpose, but then in the mornings at the center we'd sever our fresh bonds of understanding.

Back then, the questions I wanted my soul to answer were:

Was it normal for two partners to argue this much? Was it normal to moderate, or even sacrifice, a vision for the bottom line? Was it normal for someone to be constantly angry at another human being and still legitimately call herself a yogini? Was it normal to walk into a place I helped build and not feel like I belonged?

These questions were merely derivatives of the ones that had been nagging me since childhood: Was I normal, or was I a misfit, unfit to work alongside others in partnership, destined always to be an outsider? And, most importantly, did I even want to be normal since being normal seemed to curtail the perspective I had come to embrace: that life was immensely enriched by energizing the curiosity and creativity necessary for exploration of the unknown unhindered by society's norms. But muffled beneath my many roles, ambitions, and fears I could not hear my soul's reply.

## CHAPTER 41

*Control Pose*

By this time in my teaching career, all I had to do to meet the requirements of running a two-hundred-hour teacher training program was fill out paperwork. I was excited about taking a group of students through such training over a year, sharing deeper philosophical aspects of yoga than I could find time for in an hour-long class. Thankfully, gone were the weekend whirlwind teacher trainings; now it was necessary to comply with standards suggested by the Yoga Alliance, which proposed at least two hundred hours of study encompassing philosophy, ethics, lifestyle, technique, teaching methodology, anatomy and physiology, and practicum, after which students would receive their Registered Yoga Teacher (RYT-200) certificates for presentation to any yoga center or club owner. In addition, the eligibility requirements to teach others to become yoga teachers, also suggested by the Yoga Alliance, had become more stringent.

I'd never taken on such a big commitment before, along with

all my other responsibilities, so I asked a yoga teacher Meredith
had known, Angie, to assist me. Meredith had introduced me
to Angie in her kitchen one sunny winter afternoon, and, within
minutes of meeting her, I thought she was a perfect fit for our
vision. Angie agreed to teach regular classes for us and also be
my co-teacher for the yoga teacher training program, for which
Meredith, who did not yet have her RYT-200 certificate,
signed up.

Angie and I blended into something greater than our individual selves. In contrast to her physical appearance—silky,
black hair and matching eyes, olive skin, and a wardrobe con-
sisting mostly of gray shades—she was the brightest light I had
ever met. To her, I was smart, funny, and even sexy. To me, she
was effortlessly beautiful, witty, and bolder than I'd ever dared
to be. Our collaboration over yoga quickly developed into a
friendship that promised to live on into our old age. In the
classroom, Angie and I completed each other's thoughts, remembered Sanskrit words the other forgot, or explained the
same concept with just enough personal twist that everyone
nodded in understanding. Outside the classroom, whether ascending to the philosophical or descending to the ridiculous,
we understood and accepted each other unconditionally. Angie
knew about my difficulties with Meredith and was sympathetic
to my viewpoint, yet she wanted nothing to do with conflict so
urged me to live my yoga by keeping my emotions in check.

But the worsening troubles with Meredith began affecting
our teacher training class, making ignoring them more difficult.
While Meredith and I never engaged in outright accusations,

we made insinuations that only we could understand, and Meredith subtly challenged my authority and knowledge, seemingly exploiting my insecurities. In partnership meetings, Meredith would comment on the way I was running the program, always careful to state that she was speaking "as a partner not a student." For instance, she'd ask whether I was expressing favoritism in class or whether the homework was appropriate. I didn't always agree with her observations, but I tried to express gratitude for her honesty rather than bitterness over her micromanagement.

One day I shared with Angie how the constant strain between Meredith and me was waking my anxiety, making me sweat and shake in class.

"Tell her about it," Angie suggested, optimistically. "Ask her to give you some space."

"I'm afraid she'll use it against me," I hedged.

"The more she knows, the more compassion she'll have," insisted Angie.

I thought that if I revealed my ongoing anxiety issues Meredith might better understand why I needed her support in the classroom. Yet I had doubts about opening up more to Meredith at this uncertain stage in our relationship. Still, it seemed absurd under a yoga studio roof—a place where we talked constantly about authenticity, wholeness, and vulnerability—to participate in games better suited to the corporate world. As a teacher of yoga, I wanted my life to be in alignment with my teachings.

So one day I overcame my doubts and asked Meredith if

we could talk privately. We found a cozy spot in the Gathering Space, and after I shared my history of anxiety and its recent reentry in my life, I asked for personal support in the classroom. She told me how glad she was that I had revealed my concerns to her. At the time, her responses had made me feel good, but after leaving I felt uneasy and called Angie for support.

"Did Meredith listen?" she asked.

"Yes," I confirmed.

"You feel better, don't you?" Angie suggested, hoping to hear a positive response.

I answered her truthfully, "I'm not sure yet. I feel a bit exposed."

"Even in the yoga world, truth is sometimes not the best defense," said Fear, beginning to sound like the ally I was looking for.

The next week, as we all arrived for teacher training, Meredith and I waited while the students filed into the classroom. Just as we were about to enter, Meredith took my elbow and whispered, "How is your anxiety today?" Her eyes were deceptively kind, but her comment tripped me up. The deep breaths I'd taken to calm and center myself were undone in an instant. I probably tried to pretend that I was okay, but instead I should have told her the truth, that it wasn't okay. In class that day, and every week after, nothing changed between us, except the look on her face that now said, "I know your weakness."

Ultimately, the teacher training class was the challenge I had expected without the fun for which I'd hoped. When the program was over, for the sake of yoga I put my conflict with Meredith aside, signed off on her two-hundred-hour certificate, placed a bindi on her forehead, and gave her a blessing. But for the duration of this year-long program I had done what I vowed never to do again—stuffed my emotions deep inside my body, stitched a smile on my face, and practiced a pose I called Control Pose. Yet this experience taught me an important lesson: while being vulnerable and choosing to trust people with our innermost truths are important relationship-building practices, it is crucial to know with whom to be vulnerable and what information to reveal to them. Being accepted with our strengths and our weaknesses can cultivate compassion, but letting others into our lives requires vigilance and a soul's Comb of Discernment. Such invitations need to be earned rather than easily given away to the wrong people, leaving us exposed to not only physical but also mental dangers against which Control Pose cannot protect.

## CHAPTER 42

### *Megaphone of Truth*

THE RAIN FINALLY CEASES AT THE PRECIPICE, leaving behind a kaleidoscope of dancing colors more striking than any Earth Realm rainbow. Rasa pulls a gigantic, golden cone-shaped item from her tote bag and announces, "All right, my dear. We have a big-ticket item to pack." As she places the item on the lawn, it makes a twanging sound that echoes throughout the realm. The item is so tall I have to stand on tiptoe to see the top of it. It looks like an oversized bullhorn used on a sports field.

"Please," I ask tentatively, "tell me I don't have a role of coach or cheerleader in this next life?"

"Hardly, unless you want one," Rasa confirms, laughing.

"No thank you," I answer emphatically. "But tell me more about this item."

Polishing it with her pink handkerchief, she explains, "This is the megaphone of truth. You can use it in the Earth Realm to amplify your voice when you speak your truth."

I peer closer to decipher the words etched into it, which

read: "Speak your truth." Then I ask, "Is this about sharing the Great Truth?"

"No, your puzzling about the Great Truth can be done with little more than your Pen of Reflection. This is for your inner truths that must be communicated out loud in the world to a variety of people. Unlike the pen, which can help you understand yourself and the world around you, this megaphone will help you express yourself in that world."

"If it is designed to amplify my voice, couldn't I just speak louder?" I ask, even though I sense there is more to it.

She laughs and explains, "No, by amplify I do not mean your volume but rather your vibration. When you speak from a higher vibration, this megaphone will convert questions to statements. It will help you use the most precise words. It will cut out unnecessary phrases such as 'I think that,' 'I don't mean to be a bother, but,' and 'I'm sorry, but this is how I feel.' It will create fullness in the tone of your voice, without which others may not recognize the truth of your words."

"Why, the megaphone is an editor!" I say excitedly. "If it will help me speak truth more directly, it will surely calm my emotions as well."

Rasa stares at me for a moment, amused, and then says, "You're equating calmness with truth-speaking when they may or may not be connected. Calmness is not necessarily the emotions' priority." She points toward a yoga studio that has just materialized in the location where there was once a wheat field. There Fear, having exchanged his usual pinstriped suit for an electric-blue leisure suit, leads a yoga class.

"And twist! And reach! And bend!" Fear shouts.

"Fear, why are we doing this?" Anxiety squeals from his perch on the ceiling.

"I should've tried this a long time ago," Guilt says, cringing.

"You don't have the body for it, Guilt," Shame adds.

"Be quiet, everyone! I can't hear the instructions!" Anger shouts.

"I don't know, Fear. I say we give up the loincloth," Depression remarks, looking down dejectedly at his loincloth hanging loosely on him.

"Don't give up, Depression! Get back in the game!" Fear urges.

"I see what you are saying," I admit, shaking my head.

"So to be clear," Rasa continues, "the megaphone will not edit your emotions. It can, however, ensure that you will gradually become a more emotion-full person."

"Don't you mean emotional?" I say, attempting to clarify her statement using what I think is the proper Earth Realm term.

"No, I mean emotion-*full*, Sëri. When human beings are emotional, they fight against their emotions and react to circumstances in which they see themselves as victims. Emotional people are actually in denial of their emotions, so they try to get rid of them—whether by projecting them onto others, stuffing them inside their own bodies, or sending them out into the world to be felt by other poor souls simply minding their own business." She pauses then looks me straight in the eye and adds, "You will try all of these methods at various points in your coming lifetime, but none will provide the results you seek.

That is why I'm sending this megaphone with you—to help you understand and respect your emotions."

I knock on the megaphone, and the sound reverberates. I try to pick it up by its golden, S-shaped handle but soon realize that I have not yet acquired the strength, despite my many lives, to wield sufficient power.

"Do not be discouraged," Rasa says, consoling me as she takes my hand in hers. "You have managed many similar megaphones in the past, just not one quite this big. The megaphone of truth is like the robe of authority—it will take time to grow strong enough to use it."

"So practice makes perfect?" I ask, playing with my ever-deepening recollection of Earth Realm clichés. But then I see my friend's familiar raised eyebrow and know it won't be that simple.

"There is one particular business setting," she says, "where you will try picking up this megaphone of truth for the first time. But because it is new to you the words will come out too emotionally, as if its settings are too high. It is for your own growth that you experience this. Attaining perfection with this megaphone is something you can put out of your mind, but improving your ability to use it is quite possible."

"So I'm going to be emotional in a business setting, Rasa? I can sense that, though this time in my ego's life may be about growing stronger, it will not feel this way to her."

"That may be true," Rasa admits, "but what do you expect would happen when an individual who stuffs emotions tries out this megaphone of truth for the first time?"

"All the emotions, finally getting a voice, would come flying out," I answer, and she nods in agreement. "It'll probably damage relationships," I speculate, shaking my head in empathy. "You mentioned a choice between being emotional and emotion-full. Tell me, what is being emotion-full like?"

"Being emotion-full means taking responsible ownership of your emotions," Rasa explains. "Remember, all the emotions, even the difficult ones like Anger and Depression, are informers first and foremost. Their job is to warn you of danger, illness, misalignment, injustice, conflict, or betrayal. In such roles, they are not enemies but rather imperfect allies. If you can witness their neediness, observe their shortsightedness, and consider their perspectives, you will be able to respond calmly and wisely during any experience as your name Serene suggests. In such a state, you can express Anger without intentionally hurting others, notice Guilt's influence and make subtle changes without Shame intervening, and understand Fear's perspective and respond accordingly."

"It sounds simple," I muse.

"It is simple. That doesn't mean, however, that it is easy," Rasa remarks.

"But how in soulnations will this thing fit inside my suitcase?" I ask.

"You'd be amazed, Sëri, at how miraculously things can travel from the Soul Realm to the Earth Realm," Rasa replies, fitting the megaphone easily into the suitcase.

## CHAPTER 43

# *Dialogue with Soul*

AFTER MY YOGA CLASS ONE MORNING, Meredith informed me that later there would be a meeting concerning the center but withheld its purpose. In response to my audible sigh, she had said, "Just try to keep an open mind." That sounded ominous.

The meeting began in the Gathering Space with the usual pleasantries. Meredith sat to my left in a bright, full skirt and freshly applied lipstick. Next to her, across from me, was Stacy, looking polished and well-rested in her usual attire of short-sleeved shirt, pressed black pants, and lipstick. Given that those days I felt relieved if my pants weren't on backward, the lipstick offended me, like a silent message that while I was working they were playing.

"You could've at least tried to look presentable," scolded Guilt, clucking at my black yoga pants and sweatshirt.

To my right sat a middle-aged man exuding professionalism, wearing a suit and tie, with a neat haircut and trimmed nails, each with a perfect half-moon. His neatness bothered me like my partners' lipstick bothered me. He owned a dental reconstruction business about twenty minutes away, and I wondered what business he had here in the spiritual world— until he unrolled blueprints on our coffee table. My partners inched to the edges of their chairs, while I sat back, feeling more like an observer than a participant. "Here's my office, here's so-and-so's business, but this space is available," he explained. My breathing became shallow. My spine stiffened.

"An expansion," whispered Fear, ominously.

"An expansion, Keri, wake up!" echoed Anger, frantically.

The truth hit me in the gut: the others knew the purpose of this meeting but had never consulted me. For a moment, I didn't know what I was most aghast about—the expansion, the fact that my partners had deceived me, or that they thought I'd quietly relinquish the role of visionary of the center.

"Sit quietly and listen. We can fix it later," advised Fear, reluctant to cause a scene.

"They won't listen to her later! She must oppose it now," argued Anger.

"Oh, the humiliation of not having been consulted," added Shame.

I felt betrayed. Still, I'd become quite proficient at Control Pose, honing it every week around the center as I pretended that everything was just fine while it wasn't. So I pressed the pads of my fingers to my temples, pushing back Anger.

The man commented further, "You see, we have much in common! We both are in the business of helping people feel better about themselves."

If I had been drinking water, I would've spat it out. Instead, I gasped for air, for reality. I looked to my partners for validation that this man's comparison was not only ridiculous but insulting. I waited for them to explain that our center was about honoring the heart, not fixing the body. But they smiled and nodded like bobble-head dolls.

I exhaled slowly and considered what seemed like the only two options available: A) tell them what I thought about the ridiculous comparison and storm out, or B) grin and bear it. But option B, the choice I'd made again and again that usually led to hives and anxiety, was by this time no longer possible as I well knew the long-term consequences of stuffing my emotions. Speaking my truth now mattered more than whether or not these people labeled me weak or unstable. So option A it was.

"No!" I said. "We are not the same! Look, I'll show you what yoga is about!" Fueled by adrenaline and liberated rage, I grabbed one of the tank tops we had just agreed to purchase for resale, which showed the phrase "I am enough" upside down, meant only for the wearer.

"This is what yoga teaches! We don't need something outside ourselves to make us okay. We can't fix anyone because no one is broken!" I stated emphatically.

I didn't think I was shouting, but their stunned faces clued me in to what the look on mine must've been—menacing. Then I heard my daughters, who were playing nearby, giggle. In contrast to the image of me as a red-faced, wild-eyed madwoman that these adults likely had seen, my daughters had an image of me as a safe, creative, fun, caring person.

Saved by my children, I soon realized that all I would accomplish by continuing my tirade would be to justify the looks of horror on the faces of others. I put the shirt down then smoothed it out as if smoothing out my behavior. Next I did the only thing left to do: I excused myself, got my girls, and walked out, leaving my partners with a mess to clean up.

Outside in the fresh air all my emotions swarmed me like a cloud of springtime gnats. Shame admonished me for letting my partners—and a complete stranger—witness the fierce warrior side of me that I had little knowledge of or control over. Guilt criticized me for giving Anger a speaking role. Anxiety nagged me about how I would explain my actions to my partners later. Anger ranted over my partners' blindsiding. And Fear questioned my mental stability.

"I'm crazy because I believe in something and stand up for it?" I said, taking issue with Fear. "At least I know what I want, and I hold to it. What's crazier: speaking my truth or repeatedly being afraid to speak my truth? What has fear of speaking my truth gotten me in life? Only hives or depression, remember?"

"You can't let them destroy your vision for the center! This is your business, too!" shouted Anger.

"But that reaction was not normal," noted Fear.

"Or rational," added Guilt.

"Or sane," hissed Shame.

Later, during my expected phone argument with a furious Meredith, she insisted that she was as shocked as I was when the man rolled out blueprints, and it would've been nice if I could've just listened instead of throwing a tantrum. But I didn't believe her story, knowing that people at the center didn't get time on Meredith's calendar without an itinerary. The word *tantrum* triggered me, as it implied an impulsive and unimportant outburst. By contrast, my reaction, while intense, had been an authentic expression of the betrayal, shock, and anger I'd felt, neither impulsive nor unimportant. And my outburst had been effective, given the fact that after this meeting the topic of expansion was never again raised. I was convinced that no other emotion or combination of emotions could have communicated the firmness of my opposition the way Anger had.

Even so, I wished I'd acted according to an option C, treating as sacred not only my truth but also the individuals to whom I delivered it. But an option C, I can see now, would have had to begin with believing the words on the shirt I shook that day—"I am enough"—and I did not yet possess such a belief. In hindsight, I think that my soul decided to pack the seed that would lead to becoming part owner of a yoga center not because she longed to wear such a skin but because she saw in this seed something understandable only from her perspective in the realm of the soul—a growth opportunity that would move me from shouting, "I am enough" to believing it.

After the disastrous meeting and follow-up phone argument with Meredith, my body shook with confusion, anger, and self-derision. I went for a walk in the woods, where I dialogued with my soul, who was far easier to hear with me out from under my roles and identities. Our dialogue followed what I now see as a familiar pattern. First I focused on my reputation, my sense of right and wrong, and desire for safety and validation. And then my soul picked up more pieces of the Great Truth.

"If this venture fails, who will I become? An outsider, a misfit who doesn't belong anywhere?" I agonized, finally stating my greatest of all fears.

*"So . . . you want something in return for offering your gifts,"* replied my soul, encouraging me to admit that part of my effort was predicated on a desire to receive validation and acceptance from the world.

"Okay, I admit I want something in return—like building a haven from Anxiety and Depression. Is that so bad?" I answered.

*"That's understandable. But when will you stop looking outside yourself for validation? When will you really believe the words on that shirt you shook so vigorously?"* my soul challenged.

"I don't know. I want to be enough, but I also need something from this world," I confessed.

*"I think we're getting closer to the Great Truth,"* my soul stated.

"My partners think I'm losing my mind, and I'm not so sure they're wrong, yet you're contemplating the Great Truth?" I replied, annoyed at my soul's exposure of my weaknesses.

*"Thank you for this experience, Keri,"* said my soul, appreciating the lessons we both received that day.

# CHAPTER 44

## Joy's Greeting

MAIL ARRIVES IN THE SOUL REALM, heralded by the sounds of finches and cardinals. Curiosa snatches a crisp, white envelope from the air and trots over to me. I open the envelope and pull out something resembling a human greeting card. In the center of the card is a pear-shaped, pink-lipped female snake wearing a flowing white skirt and blouse, an oversized candy-pink coat, a frilly white hat, and jingling jewelry. This emotion, Joy, has written a note with a pink coloring wand, which I read out loud for Rasa and Curiosa:

*Dearest Serene Voyager,*

*You must be anticipating my arrival, as time is growing short before your departure for the Earth Realm. Alas, upon receiving my trip itinerary it has come to my attention that I will not be joining you until much later in your human journey. So I write to inform you that my protégés,*

Happiness and Laughter, will assist you through the years when you are growing up as you savor home-cooked food, dwell in the beauty of nature, develop your body's strength and agility, travel to distant places in your dreams, and connect at a deep level with other human beings on what is to be a soulful journey.

Therefore, please do not despair. My delay in joining you will make our reunion all the sweeter! Then we will delve further into the richness of life, experience authenticity and wholeness, learn the value of friends and family, and seek purpose and meaning. Never again will love be something conditional. Never again will you feel a duty to find work of which others approve. Together we will wholly and consciously engage in the world without waiting for permissions, reasons, excuses, credentials, titles, office spaces, classrooms, or platforms. Through our work together, we will shine such a bright light into the world that my sometimes-reclusive sisters, Gratitude and Contentment, will not be able to resist joining us.

It is likely that by the time we meet you will have been searching for me for some time. You may have ideas about how to find me based on what you've learned from movies, books, or spiritual teachings. But unlike what you may have learned, I am not a simple emotion that can be manifested and discarded at will. Rather, I am a cultivated *emotion, grown in the soil of steady and mindful efforts and intentions.*

*I have reviewed your map of opportunities, on which all that stands between us is a thin band of tall, protective trees called the forest of hardship, which you must traverse to get to me. You may be confused about how hardship could lead to joy, but hardship is a part of human life. And, to experience joy, it is necessary for every embodied soul to experience suffering. In the Earth Realm, it is only through the duality of suffering and joy that the expanded consciousness you seek can occur. So, dear soul, navigate your way through the forest of hardship, and I will be there waiting.*

*In anticipation of our future together,*
*Joy*

At Joy's note, my heart feels alternately heavy and light, knowing I will have to undergo a trial before Joy arrives and that ultimately I will experience this emotion in my next life in the Earth Realm.

## Chapter 45

### Numb

"You don't belong at the center anymore," a trusted confidante said as we shared a cup of tea together in her living room. With love shining from her eyes and tears glistening in mine, she spoke the truth I hadn't been willing to say to myself, in words I'd dreaded my entire life: you don't belong. My instinct was to prove the words, and the decision that would logically follow, were wrong. My emotions piled on.

"If you walk away, you will be humiliated," opined Shame.

"If you walk away, you will be an outsider, and this failure will follow you wherever you go," warned Fear.

"If you walk away, I will be waiting for you," Depression said.

"As will I," warned Anxiety.

*"As will I,"* promised my soul.

Bolstered by the promise of my soul, I contemplated the implications of leaving the center, picturing my life without conflict, instead able to read books, plan family vacations, and spend evenings with family in lieu of doing financial reports. Considering this, I started to breathe deeper as the meaning of the words *you don't belong* changed from something I feared would cause pain to something that could set me free.

Once I decided to leave the center the next problem was how to announce it to my partners. Given our deteriorated relationship, I didn't feel I could do it in person, so I sent a carefully worded resignation email on Valentine's Day, which doubled as an act of self-love, clicking "send" with a sense of reclaiming some lost power. I didn't pretend that my departure was for any reason other than the unhealthy partnership and diverging visions, but I expressed sadness that I could see no viable future together. My email was met with silence, and Meredith feigned surprise to students and staff—as if there had been no warning sign. Only after I was gone and had hired a lawyer to write letters on my behalf did I receive official acknowledgment, through Meredith's lawyer, claiming I had made my decision "on a whim." It was a challenge to my own perception of reality. But I, as well as my family and the students who had left when I had, knew the truth.

I led my final class at the center against a wall I had painted, sitting on flooring I had helped select, and facing students I called friends, who expressed both sadness and bewilderment at my decision. To leave with a modicum of civility, all I told them was that it was time for me to move on.

"But are you still going to teach?" they asked.

"I don't know yet," I answered truthfully.

After my final class, Meredith cheerfully greeted everyone

312 Embodying Soul

as if I were going on vacation somewhere warm. She no longer reminded me of a cardinal but of a hawk, scoping out new territory. While I packed, she tried to say something, but I was finally able to calmly and unequivocally tell her I didn't want to hear it.

As I walked out to my car, Fear taunted, "Perhaps you weren't spiritual enough to make this vision work. Now you will be an outsider again, unwelcome in the very spiritual community you helped build."

"I'd rather be an outsider and free than shackled to something that causes me pain," I countered and meant it.

But I still had questions for my soul.

"What will my life look like without a yoga studio, without a title and purpose, without an identity?" I asked, seeing no path to my future.

*"Imagine the freedom!"* my soul replied,
seeing it from a broader perspective.

"Will I become insignificant?" I asked, still concerned.

*"You have regained your self-respect.
That is worth more than significance,"* replied my soul.

"But I loved teaching yoga and saw it as my life's purpose. I was going to further pursue truth at the center," I protested.

*"You don't need the center or these particular roles to
continue our pursuit of truth,"* my soul reminded me.
*"As in your relationship with books, you must now see*

*the evolutionary purpose this human skin served in your life
and move on to a new beginning.
Use the Pen of Reflection and see for yourself just how many
truths you have collected in such a short time."*

"Okay, I'll try to see what I've learned," I agreed.

Upon reflection, I was amazed to realize that I now understood many truths about my ego and my soul. First I learned that my ego was deeply afraid to offer "just myself" to the world—without credentials, office space, or a service. I had treated the center as an extension of myself, and let its growth and direction define me, which is why its departure from my original vision hurt so much. Then I remembered that my soul was not on this planet, and in this body, to be a cog in the wheel for anyone else or for a business in which I didn't believe. I wanted to invent, to create, to explore. And I wanted a life with my soul, not one beholden to my ego.

Yet despite gaining meaningful insights I still had to accept the loss of my hodgepodge identity as spiritual teacher, business owner, and entrepreneur, roles that had given me self-worth and a sense of value in society. It was Anxiety who brought this message when, one day while I was pacing in the garden, he asked: "What if you find no other great purpose for the rest of your life? What if this was all just a waste of time?"

I picked some weeds, traipsed to the backyard, and complained, "You're going to exhaust me with your what ifs, Anxiety."

"Okay, instead let's do a jigsaw puzzle, which we can control," suggested Anxiety, his red eyes turning to the dining room cabinet where I stored puzzles.

"Then what do we do after the puzzle?" I asked.

"Fix something broken, like change out lightbulbs," replied Anxiety.

"Anxiety, it's crucial that I try to mourn this loss," I insisted, aware of the necessity for grieving in order to move forward.

"I can't let go enough yet," replied Anxiety.

"Keri, can I get you anything?" interrupted my husband, seeing me anxiously pacing.

"Can you bring me a glass of red wine," I replied, tempted by Depression's cloak of empty calories.

"Do you want to go for a walk first?" he suggested.

"I can't now. My body is numb. Please bring the wine," I answered.

Consumed by Anxiety and tempted by Depression's cloak of empty calories, I began to neglect my family and social life, even forgetting to call my mom on Mother's Day, which required many apologies. I didn't want to talk with anyone associated with the center, both because I didn't want them to take pity on me and because I had no love left for them. I was like a trapped wolf; anyone who reached out a helping hand, except for a few trusted friends, was likely to get it bitten off. I had learned my lesson about speaking my truth to people who hadn't earned the right to hear it, and I now swung to another extreme: I stopped trusting people with any information about me and ceased believing in their concern for me, convinced that people cared about no one except themselves. I lost all faith in humanity.

I didn't answer emails, make calls, teach, or practice yoga. I was only able to tend to my new puppy, a Cavalier King Charles spaniel I named Charlie. During our first week together, Charlie and I cuddled for long periods on the couch, him wallowing in his recent neutering and me in the loss of my purpose. Ultimately, daily walks with Charlie in nature became a crucial part of my healing, although I was upset upon noticing Meredith walking by my house, her body language reflecting her certainty about her right to do so. There was nothing illegal about her walking by my house, but I felt stalked and feared that I would meet her on some solitary stretch of road where we could not ignore each other. I wanted to go into hiding so I could heal. But every day I had to drive past the center to go to the grocery store. Thus my early healing was like trying to mend a broken arm while continuing to fall on it.

While beginning this business, I had hoped to set aside my yang, fiery self and let the watery yin yoga shift the décor of my mind into cooler, softer hues. But instead I had relearned the value and purpose of yang as my soul showed me that my yang warrior self, not my yin philosophical self, would thaw the numbness of victimhood and spur me to reclaim all the power I'd lost, and then some. The warrior and the yogini, I concluded, could together wrap me in the resolve I needed and the mindfulness I craved to feel deeply for the sake of a future, more integrated self.

# PART VII

## *Sensation*

❧

The skin, with its network of nerves,
is highly sensitive to both pleasure and pain.
The skin can tingle, crawl, break out in goose bumps,
burn, or glow. Skin, porous and receptive,
allows us to intimately experience the world around us
through touch, the first human language.
The skin's scars, patterns, and wrinkles
reveal a history of sensation that can remind us
of our past or portend our future.
The skin's confines, paradoxically,
allow us to dream of more expansive states
beyond the body—a realm of the soul.

## CHAPTER 46

### *Pierced*

OVER THE NEXT FEW MONTHS, dealing with the aftermath of my departure from the center took many twists and turns that tested both my resilience and my trust in people, ultimately bringing me closer to my family, to empathy for humanity, and to my soul. These gains began, however, with more loss. One day Angie texted me an invitation for coffee, our Friday ritual for months, and I typed the message, one heartbreaking letter after the next: "I think it's time we let each other go." Once I'd pressed "send," though, I muttered a wish that she would suggest some way we could still be friends, even though she was staying at the center and I was moving on. But her text back read: "I understand. I agree." At that moment, I knew our friendship was truly over. There would be no more ascending to the philosophical or descending to the ridiculous. For weeks I had tried to hold on to our friendship. Some days I had attempted to hide my pain around her, to prove to her that I'd moved on, wanting her to be proud of me. Other days I had expressed anger over my belief that the center had been *my* dream and Meredith had stolen it. Angie had told me I should admit that Meredith was a very influential woman and give her credit for all she had brought to the center. I had told Angie that I wasn't ready for forgiveness or understanding, that honoring my own heart came first. But the energy between us had become increasingly tense. She had admitted that at times she had purposely said things to trigger my anger and wasn't sure why. I didn't understand how someone who said she loved me could do that unless her loyalty had shifted away from me to the center. But I knew I had every right to stand up for my healing and my truth and that leaving this friendship, as heartbreaking as it was, would be a way to reclaim those valuable aspects of myself.

As I was sitting on the bed sobbing about the loss of Angie's friendship, my young girls, eight and ten, bounded into the room and stared at me, making me wonder how I could explain this to them. I knew that if the scene had been playing out between my mom and me, my mom would've told me that nothing was wrong, but that would've made me feel undervalued and deceived. So I invited my girls up on the bed next to me and, holding my heart, said, "I just broke up with my best friend, Angie." I explained how hard we had tried to hang on to our friendship, to leave the past behind, to be happy for each other as our paths diverged, but that finally I'd had to admit I was not a big enough person to be happy for her new-found opportunities resulting from my departure from the center.

Surprisingly, my girls were able to understand, without

diminishing my pain by saying, "But you've known her only a year," or encouraging me to seek the silver lining by reminding me how "those conversations were getting really awkward." They hugged my pain away as I cried on their shoulders like a colicky baby, reminding myself never to underestimate their ability for compassion because of their youth. On the contrary, perhaps it was their youth that enabled them to offer compassion in a way that others, seeing my situation as only a lost job, could not. I was saved by my children yet again.

The next healing salve I experienced came from my husband, who knew nothing of healing mantras, aromatherapies, or New Age forgiveness techniques. One day while fuming over having seen Meredith at the grocery store and hidden behind a rack of bakery items to avoid a confrontation with her, I was slicing sweet red peppers with the kind of vigor needed for raw butternut squash when my husband suddenly said, "Keri, repeat after me: 'Fuck that.'"

"I don't think I can," I replied with a frown, trying to smother a smile.

"Try," he insisted, eyes trained on me with passion.

One might think that a woman who screams at full volume in a car can say, "Fuck that" without much trouble. But the scream had been impulsive, while swearing out loud would be a conscious choice that flew in the face of my goodness-me, oh-golly upbringing and also leave no doubt as to whether I was reaching for enlightenment or getting down in the mud to wrestle human demons. Yet I put down the knife and, looking down, said, "Fuck that."

"Louder," my husband coached.

"Fuck that!" I shouted, looking straight at him.

"Again!" he commanded.

"Fuck that!" I screamed, pounding my fist on the counter. We both laughed, then I cried and he hugged me.

"Let's work on healing together, one day at a time," Todd said, putting his hands on my shoulders and looking me in the eyes. "I love you. I want to help. This family loves you and needs you," he added. Minutes later, all cried out, I returned to slicing the peppers, more gently this time.

Weeks later Anger challenged me, saying, "Your blind love for yoga was likely to blame. You gave your heart to it, and look where it got you! Yoga might be all well and good in the Himalayas but not here in the real world."

"Yes, Anger. My blind love for yoga and also the shallow world were at fault," I begrudgingly agreed.

"Those hypocrite yoga teachers at the center did not speak up for you or leave in solidarity. Sure, some have stayed in touch, but most have just forgotten about you," Anger continued.

"Right! If they had cared about me, they would've stood up for me!" I agreed.

"There's one more target," hissed Anger. "Your soul."

"What?" I replied, chewing my lip. But it didn't take long to see that I was, in fact, angry at my soul, the part of me that was supposed to be wise about things. I was angry at her disappearing act during the most difficult times at the center, which had been my soul's idea in the first place. So I turned to her, demanding explanations.

"Because I listened to you, I'm no longer a yoga teacher or a business partner. I have no purpose, no value, and am making no contribution. Everyone's always talking about following their souls, but I followed you straight to failure. Because of you, I am nothing, as I always feared," I said accusingly to my soul.

*"Are you so sure? We are free to explore this world together.*
*I've never felt so embodied in this lifetime,"*
countered my soul.

"You keep saying I'm free, but I'm a hermit. I can't even go out for coffee without fear of running into someone who will ask me what happened," I argued.

*"Have patience. Everything in time. Joy is close,"*
said my soul, encouragingly.

"I'm as far away from Joy as any human being could be. Explain to me why this experience has hurt so much and for so long. People lose businesses all the time and go on to the next chapter in their lives hardly blinking an eye. Why can't I?" I implored.

*"This isn't about a lost business. This is about learning lessons*
*and increasing consciousness. This is about living your yoga.*
*There is a grand opportunity for evolution before us,"*
my soul insisted.

"No one in their right mind would look at this mess and call it an opportunity," I commented.

*"That is because I am not in your mind.*
*That's where Fear lives. I live in your heart,"*
said my soul.

"Exactly. I have a great pain in my heart partly because my partners who betrayed me are probably celebrating getting me out of the center with wine and dancing," I accused.

*"Do you not wonder if your partners might have expected*
*more from you, if you are not only victim but also perpetrator,*
*or if none of you understood the fear and desire*
*cloaked by your virtuous endeavor?*
*If you want to truly understand the external betrayal,*
*you must look further inward, while simultaneously*
*expanding your perspective on the situations of others,"*
my soul insisted.

"I don't have the energy for your paradoxes," I complained. "Besides, I never betrayed myself."

*"Is that so? Where's Curiosa?"* my soul asked.

"She's a wild animal. I cannot schedule or predict her comings and goings," I replied defensively, aware that I had again stopped nurturing my curiosity.

Nor was this the only way I had betrayed myself. I had betrayed my commitment to self-care as I let my pain begin to define me. I had taken my body for granted as I assumed, like I had so many times before, it would do my bidding while I chased after rewards. I had betrayed my heart's longing for freedom of creativity and my soul's desire for adventure and exploration. And my abrupt departure from the center had hurt and confused others. These were the pieces of awareness I needed to progress to the next phase of my healing, which would involve refining my communication with my emotions and soul, while expanding my vision from my own limited viewpoint to that of others.

## CHAPTER 47
### *Puzzling Gratitude*

THE TIME OF DEPARTING ON MY JOURNEY DRAWS NEAR, and my hands will not stop fidgeting nor my feet stop pacing. Rasa hands me a boxed game and says, "Here, this will calm your nerves and be good practice!"

I sit on the grass, open the box, and shake it, causing a thousand tiny cardboard pieces to fall to the ground. With delight, I say, "Oh, I love puzzles! What is this one a picture of?"

"This is no ordinary puzzle. This is a healing puzzle. Snapped into place, each piece will bring you closer to the understanding needed to pass through the forest of hardship," Rasa explains.

"How do I put together a puzzle without knowing what it should look like?" I ask.

"Lay out all the pieces and just begin," advises Rasa.

I explore the many pieces, some with smooth, rounded edges; others with rough, scalloped edges; still others square. On the face of each piece there is color and shape, but no single piece provides meaning. I begin with a frame of edge pieces. Then I organize the remaining pieces by color, shape, and size. Finally, I fill in the middle, section by section. Eventually, with patience and fortitude, I click the final piece into place. Curiosa, watching over my shoulder, yelps with approval. All three of us move back so we can take in the likeness of a graceful, radiant, emerald green snake, her curved figure wrapped in tinkling bracelets of gold, her smile radiating light, presence, and joy.

"Gratitude," I murmur. "I would recognize her anywhere."

Just then I feel cool breath on my shoulder. I turn to find the usually blue-faced Fear turned stark white, staring at Gratitude with awe.

"Does she frighten you, Fear?" I ask.

"I…well, she's stunning," answers Fear, his voice trembling.

"That she is. Perhaps we will meet her someday along our journey," I reply. I adjust Fear's black fedora as he continues staring at Gratitude for several moments, his mouth gaping, his eyes unblinking. Finally, he blinks rapidly to pull himself out of his reverie and grumbles, "But she doesn't look very ambitious," before slinking away.

Rasa and I exchange a questioning look. "Could Gratitude be the partner that Fear, who lives life as if danger lurks around every corner, needs most in my ego's life? And could the presence of Gratitude help quell Anxiety, too?" I ask.

"That might be," says Rasa, hinting at a possible lesson for my ego in the Earth Realm.

"Oh, I hope so," I remark, as I pack the healing puzzle in my suitcase in anticipation of Gratitude playing an important role in the healing of my ego, so often driven by Fear and Anxiety.

## CHAPTER 48

*Awakening*

ARMED WITH NOTHING BUT OYSTER CRACKERS, I arrived at a restaurant to meet with Stacy and negotiate a plan to legally get me out of the business. After attempts over the last months to negotiate my exit through lawyers had failed, after my partners had pulled out of a scheduled arbitration meeting, and after continuous accusations, my naïveté was gone and I had the broader perspective of a mature businesswoman who would never again let blind faith be the only currency in which she traded. One reason we hadn't been able to come to closure earlier was that the other partners had asked me to sign a non-compete agreement, which I opposed as it could have given them power to dictate my future choices. In addition, the idea of Meredith, who had obtained her yoga teacher training certificate from me, trying to stop me from teaching yoga seemed an affront to the freedom for which yoga stood. So it had looked like the only thing left to do was go to court, a solution no one wanted, though I had little left to lose.

"What's the worst that could happen if we go to court?" I had asked my lawyer.

"The judge could order that the business be dismantled if the three of you can't come to terms," she had answered, and I thought, angrily, bring it on. Finally, though, Stacy and I had agreed to see what just the two of us could negotiate. I knew this meeting would be our last chance to agree on terms, but I also realized that it was important to speak up for myself.

Stacy was waiting for me at a table for two. She looked battle-weary, making me think that rather than celebrating my exit with wine and dance the others had probably found the increased workload more difficult than I could ever know. The insight made me wince with embarrassment.

With obvious tension between us, Stacy opened the conversation while I opened my bag of oyster crackers and popped a few in my mouth. I started to reply but instead spit out a spray of cracker crumbs. We both laughed, which diffused the tension like air leaked from a balloon. I felt genuine appreciation for her willingness to talk to me. We smiled at each other, no longer enemies on separate sides of a battlefield tossing grenades of demands and accusations but two women in a tight spot that neither of us would have chosen.

Being more empathetic than before, we examined the situation through each other's eyes. Stacy's affirmation that I wasn't the only person to blame, that there were three of us who could've done better, allowed me to reclaim some dignity. Her candor helped cut through some false expectations as she told me I would never get any money back for the simple reason that the company did not have enough money. No longer privy to the company's financial situation yet aware it had been through nearly a year of legal bills, I believed she was being honest. Though initially it had seemed fair to ask for my full investment back, by this time I had come to the same conclusion as Stacy. But I asked for the return of personal belongings such as the furniture I had brought to the center.

"They are only things," the yogini in me argued, urging me to display my spiritual progress by not showing attachment to them.

"But they are my things, and I want them back," the businesswoman in me overruled. Stacy agreed to my request with a simple nod.

Finally, we addressed the mortgage, the stickiest aspect. Fortunately, I learned that my ex-partners had found new investors to take my place on the mortgage. All we had to do was work out the details and sign some paperwork. Within minutes, Stacy and I were able to resolve the issues that had been stumbling blocks for almost a year, a feat I attributed to our human connection, our mutual ability to momentarily set our own hurts aside and listen to each other empathetically.

Sometimes, with a glass of wine in my hand and memories rising like the tide in my mind, I return to this three-year period in my life, not to reexperience the pain but because I had taken on and thrown off so many roles in such a short time that it has taken years to incorporate the lessons of each into my life. I have learned that we cannot shift from suffering to gratitude and forgiveness in one healing session, one day, or one month. The deeper the pain, the longer the healing takes, no matter how earnestly we attend to it. True healing requires an honest admission about where we are, not buying into illusions of where we think we should be. True healing necessitates allowing it to naturally progress without insisting it occur according to some imaginary timeline. True healing demands we see our pain in the context of our own lives rather than in comparison to another's pain. I realized that we know healing has occurred when a memory stings less, when an incident does not take up so much space in our minds, when we can look back at an experience and chuckle at our own blindness.

Regarding the yoga business, what I had been blind to but now could see was that to believe my dream of having a center of mindfulness grounded in a shared purpose had been stolen was to give my power away. Very little in this world is within our control, particularly outcomes, but whether we speak out or acquiesce along the way, whether we create or mimic, whether we question or accept are well within our control. A path of awareness is not an easy path or one likely to be accompanied by lights and bliss, but it is an authentic path.

Finally, I now could see that instead of holding the vision of a center of mindfulness in the safekeeping of my soul and letting it emerge slowly while considering alternatives, I had been in a hurry to manifest it so had let my ego run with it. I had wanted much in return for planting the seed—happiness, security, joy, approval, and acceptance—so my motives had not been as altruistic as I had wanted to believe. Jesus once said, "Don't give pearls to swine"; I would add "Don't give seeds of creation to your ego."

As a new dawning arrived, tiny letting gos occurred inside me daily. Stability and peace returned to my life. The adage "This is the first day of the rest of your life" felt true. I felt hope for the future, now having all the necessary soul tools to reengage with the world, and I was ready to again feel both the pain and the pleasure of life.

## CHAPTER 49

# Guilt's Epiphany

As the time of my journey to the Earth Realm grows ever closer, Contentment appears, her lush, curvy snake body draped in elegant, soft white, flowing fabric. Her eyes dazzle with a hypnotic crimson glow. Her hair is adorned with rubies, diamonds, and emeralds that sparkle in the light. Carrying only a single white bag, Contentment does not exude the extravagance or boldness of Joy. Nor does she have much of anything to say. Contentment just *is*. Contentment is wise and old, yet no one would guess her age from her youthful appearance. Even Anxiety, staring from a safe distance, is impressed by her breathtaking beauty.

Perplexed by this vision of grace, Guilt lumbers out from underneath the settee and demands, "Where are her rules and lists? What must God think of the approach to life that Contentment instills?" Guilt stares transfixed by Contentment's eyes, which know the truth behind Guilt's motivations—hidden fears, desperate longings, and broken dreams.

"Guilt," I say, "we can only hope to find Contentment somewhere on the map of opportunities, to experience greater peace."

"She resides just beyond the clearing of joy, past the oasis of gratitude," reveals Rasa.

As he observes Contentment, Guilt experiences his first-ever epiphany: behind Contentment's sparkling wise eyes the road to divinity surely lies.

## CHAPTER 51

### *Harvest of Joy*

FIVE YEARS AFTER ESTABLISHING THE YOGA CENTER, I strolled through the overgrown grass of a park bordering a lake. Staring out across open water, I took some of the deepest breaths I had taken in several years. By now, after another move—this time from the suburbs to the city—I had experienced forgiveness of myself and others and had begun to again feel my soul's craving for the companionship of other people, relishing the prospect of participating once more in the rainbow of life.

But I still had a concern about whether life would take me back. While looking at the tree-lined trail before me, I felt a cold jolt as Fear slithered up my spine. "When did the world grow so big and so busy? What if we don't belong?" Fear said, pointing his nose at the people around us—sweet couples, laughing families, moms pushing strollers with sleeping babies, bikers pedaling furiously, children writing notes to the magical elf living in the ash tree, an old man reading contentedly on a bench.

I wondered if I could allow myself to again chance rejection. "How are you feeling, Fear, about interacting with others again, without a job or even a future plan on our horizon?" I asked.

"I don't know how to feel secure without a reputation holding me up," he admitted. "And I don't know if I'm ready to let the need for approval go."

"Let's practice what we've learned, Fear: when you decide that you are enough, the suffering, striving, and needing will fall away like old skins," I suggested, handing him a silver vial with a tiny amount of liquid inside.

"Keri, you have Compassion for me?" he asked, touched.

Fear swallowed a bit of Compassion, loosened his tie, then smiled and asked, "What's that new emotion I sense arriving?"

As my five senses scrambled to collect data and carry it
to my brain for interpretation, my soul announced,
*"Her name is Joy, Keri."*

"She's here for me? Then tell me how I court her," I asked.

*"Just look up,"* advised my soul.

As I raised my head, a woman about my age walked toward me and smiled, and I returned the smile spontaneously—without wanting anything, with only a desire for connection. After her smile invited me back to life, I shared my own with the next person and the next. Men, women, children, even dogs smiled back at me. When I encountered people who didn't, whose brows were knitted in worry, I had compassion for them as I now had for myself. Greeting by greeting, I experienced Joy simply through my willing presence. I was just a woman taking a walk. I was no longer a woman with a lost business; or a woman who had once believed in a grand idea; or a woman with kids or a husband; or a woman with a degree or a mission; or even a woman who had earned her right to take up space through worldly success. I was more fully alive in the here and now than I'd ever been chasing after roles or goals.

The summer breeze raised goose bumps on my skin. The sun warmed my neck. Desire to run and leap along the shoreline sparked inside me, and then, just as I turned the last bend for home, I saw her.

First, her huge, silver head poked out from between the trees, her moon-shaped eyes giving me the look I deserved. I watched as her long, sinewy legs cut through the air, stretching farther than any earthly wolf could dream. She landed by my feet, her lips drawn back to display two rows of sharp white teeth, her wildness inciting my wildness, her curiosity feeding my curiosity. Curiosa was back where she belonged. I rubbed my nose against her wet, black one as she growled with contentment.

"Have you heard of Ayurveda, Curiosa?" I whispered in my lifelong companion's ear. "It's yoga's sister science. While yoga offers self-realization, Ayurveda focuses on self-healing. If we study Ayurveda, we can learn about herbs, oils, diet, bodywork, and many other healing techniques. What do you say?"

Curiosa howled for yes. Then, flanked by Curiosa and Joy,

I continued my walk, reflecting on the notion that maybe we don't have to earn joy. Maybe when we cease trying so hard, being so much to so many, comparing ourselves to everyone else, Joy just appears, ready for us to gobble her up like raspberry ice cream topped with chocolate sauce and wild, fresh-picked huckleberries.

## CHAPTER 51

### *The Beginning*

STANDING AT THE EDGE OF THE PRECIPICE, I stare down at the rushing River of Forgetting. My feet itch with anticipation. I imagine slipping into smooth, human skin once again and watching, through human eyes, the wind juggle bright fall leaves while the cool, evening breeze brings goose bumps to my new skin. I can already see myself leaping barefoot along the shoreline, leaving marks of my presence behind for only moments before they are erased by the elements and I, too, slip back into watery oneness, returning to the Soul Realm.

My travel guide takes my hands in hers and gives some last words of advice: "As you begin your journey, fully swathed in truth and love, anything you experience that is even a salt shake less will act as a binding, limiting your freedom and movement in the world. Do not fret, for if you did not feel constrained or outcast in some way, you would never search for freedom. If you did not have some sense of discontent, in-

completeness, even suffering, you would not commit to searching for the Great Truth. And if you continue fighting for the
freedom to explore your life without boundaries you will learn
a great lesson: the human quest for freedom, authenticity, and
truth is simultaneously beautiful and painful, harrowing and
fruitful."

"It's the paradox of life," I muse at the wonder of it.

"Yes, but above all," she whispers, "regardless of how many
times you forget who you are beneath the confusing layers of
human skins you are never abandoned. Nothing you do can
cause you to be forgotten, neglected, or rejected. No matter
where in the universe you go, it will always be within your power
to receive the gifts of the Soul Realm, the place where you will
always belong."

Wrapped in blankets of divine light, feeling strong and
capable, I press a finger against the flame-shaped print on my
suitcase to seal it for the journey.

"Oh, wait!" Rasa says, opening her magical tote bag a final
time and handing me a pair of pink jelly shoes. They are a children's size twelve. "Take them as a reminder to always, no matter what, believe like a child."

We both laugh and shed tears of joy. "Rasa," I say, my soul
body swelling with gratitude, "it is impossible to thank you for
all that you have done."

"My dear friend," she replies, shaking her head. "I suspect
one day soon you will be helping me pack, for this is the cir-
cular nature of our relationship. In fact, once my Soul Animal

Shelter is established I would like to try on some human skins again in the Earth Realm, and I cannot imagine a finer travel guide than you, Sëri."

"It would be my honor," I say and gently kiss her good-bye.

I slip the pink jelly shoes on my feet and pick up my dandelion-yellow suitcase with bears on the covering. Then I, Serene Voyager, dive toward the River of Forgetting with Endless Curiosity in flight by my side to merge with my ego and journey with her toward greater truth, increased consciousness, and soul embodiment.

## CHAPTER 52

## *Choosing a Life Led by Soul*

DURING A 2011 EVENT FOCUSED ON women's empowerment, held in Boulder Colorado, a woman who had just led a workshop announced, "Before you go to lunch, reach beneath your seat. You'll each find an envelope that holds a message from your soul."

Given the wise insights and inspiring stories I'd heard during the workshop the past few days, I felt confident my soul message would be perfectly tailored to me. I opened the envelope, unfolded a single page torn from a magazine, and hunted front and back for a picture of something that would reveal an important insight, guide me to a must-read book, or show me an image of a woman grounded in her body with light shining from her eyes, mirroring the soul embodiment I had felt these past days. But all I could see were photos of kitchen displays and a list of shopping tips. Amidst cries of "I knew it!" and "Just what I needed to hear!" around me, I felt disappointed. I folded the page back up and prepared to toss it in my bag. But then

I heard the by now unmistakable voice of my soul advising me.

"*Look closer,*" implored my soul.

Feeling my fingers tingle, I did as my soul suggested. This time when I looked at the page a single word popped out: *travel.* Why hadn't I seen that the first time? I wondered. Then I scanned all the pictures again, which were of kitchen displays in shops of Charleston, South Carolina, accompanied by a brief article entitled "A Perfect Day." My heart skipped a beat as I considered the potential message for me.

"*What do you say we go on an adventure with your family
to experience a perfect day in Charleston?*"
suggested my soul. "*After all,
what is life about if not adventure, wonder, and passion?*"

"Ah, adventure, wonder! Oh, my soul, it's been so long since I've taken a spontaneous vacation like this," I said.

"*Keri, what if you called me by my name from this point on,*"
my soul suggested.

"You have a name as a soul?" I asked, surprised.

"*Many souls have names. Mine is Serene Voyager,
because of our love of travel and adventure
and the equanimity with which we attempt to
understand this human journey—
Sëri for short, which rhymes with Keri.
And you know my companion, Curiosa,
whose full name is Endless Curiosity.*"

*Soon you will meet my soul friend Rasa,*
*who cared for Curiosa at her Soul Animal Shelter*
*during your troubling times in the Earth Realm,"*
my soul explained.

"I always suspected Curiosa was partnered with me to encourage my curiosity and that someone was taking care of her when she wasn't with me," I said. "Because no matter how long she was gone she always returned to me as strong as ever."

*"Which reminds me. I have quite a story to tell you*
*about my time before our joining and communication,*
*a story that will give you insight into*
*your real home in the Soul Realm.*
*Would you like to hear it?"* she asked.

"Yes, of course! But how will I understand Soul Realm language?"

*"What knowledge I have is yours*
*if you consciously drop down into your body.*
*For then, the soul is no longer contained within*
*the body and mind, but the body and mind*
*are contained within the soul."*

"You're speaking of embodiment," I said, remembering our many intimate conversations in which she'd explained these things to me. "Sëri, I do understand your longing for embodiment, and appreciate the empowerment that comes from it. But the idea of disconnecting through enlightenment will always appeal to me," I admitted. "Flying away seems so much easier."

*"When I leapt into the River of Forgetting to join you*
*in this lifetime, I never hoped for easy.*
*I longed for adventure, and lessons, and the opportunity*
*for growth through taking on and off various human skins.*
*I said yes to this life, knowing all that it can entail.*
*We can do this together. But first, can we go on that trip?"*
she asked again.

"Impatience is not something I would normally associate with a soul," I teased.

*"There is no state of being that is hidden from me.*
*Like human skins, emotions, experiences, and roles do not*
*define me and cannot contain me,"* my soul answered.

"Is that a Great Truth?" I asked.

*"Yes, indeed. Keri, I am hopeful that a trip like this*
*can give us a good starting point for a deeper connection*
*between us,"* she said lovingly.

"You're assuming that I trust you again," I said.

*"Do you?"* my soul asked.

I thought about it. I knew by this time that choosing a life led by my soul—by Serene Voyager—and our often-unwieldy emotional companions was no less risky than a life led by my ego. But I had no more illusions that a life aligned with my soul would automatically lead to a life of peace, acceptance, or any other earthly or spiritual measure of accomplishment. I understood that Depression was a bit right about this world being an ugly, unjust place where rejection awaits. I was aware that choosing to live my life awake in communion with my soul did not assure I would never face more hives or anxiety attacks, or that my ego's patterns of critical self-doubt and stubborn independence would never plague me again. But something important had changed: now my journey was motivated not by a desperation to know but by an endless curiosity to seek. "Serene Voyager, let's go on that adventure, and the next one, too," I affirmed, thrilled to recommit to a life of adventure, wonder, and passion with my soul.

# Epilogue
## The Great Truth (Revisited)

AS TIME PASSED, MY INCREASED DESIRE FOR CONNECTION with others, ability to experience compassion, and stronger bond with my soul ultimately allowed me to care lovingly for my mother physically and emotionally when she needed vertebrae surgery, unlike during her earlier kidney transplant surgery, when I was fifteen hundred miles away in Oregon—broke, unemployed, and too filled with fear and shame to be of service to anyone. My mom's kidney had lasted for some twenty years, but the Prednisone, which she had been required to have every day since the operation, had taken its toll on her bones, requiring surgery on her vertebrae. My yoga training had taught me how to adjust my mom's feet and legs into a position that took pressure off her lower back and to calm her by helping her breathe deeply when she took a first painful walk down the hospital hallway. And while my mom recovered, my steady presence allowed my dad to gradually emerge from his cocoon of stress and worry, pleased that their home did not need to be made wheelchair accessible. We talked together excitedly about possible vacations and freedom in their retirement years.

My new perspective also helped me better appreciate the situation of the attending nurse, perhaps in her late twenties, who was kind, knowledgeable, and had answered all our questions patiently. She explained, while checking my mom's vitals and fluid levels, that prior to earning her RN degree she had received two additional undergraduate degrees, one of which was in kinesiology, saying with a chuckle, "But now I feel it's time to leave school and gain some real-world experience."

My dad, having returned to his congenial self now that my mom was recovering, thoughtfully remarked, "But none of that was wasted time, was it?"

"Oh no, not at all," she replied, shaking her head.

The remark sparked reflection on how, during my younger years, the fear of wasting time had been like a drumbeat, pushing me continuously on even when my body was suffering. Now, as an adult with a handful of failed ventures behind me and no new ideas on the horizon, I felt my dad's question lodge in my mind. Though my own life trajectory so far could be seen, through society's lens, as wasted time, I now believed that on life's journey there were no wrong turns, just a series of new beginnings, some of which could be discerned only in hindsight. I also realized, perhaps to my young self's dismay, that I might not cross a single finish line but would continue to stand before many new beginnings with endless curiosity.

Thanks to communication with my soul, I now knew that one of humanity's greatest fallacies was thinking there was some perfect, right formula for life. After all, our human journey does not follow a linear path from A to Z; rather, each of us has a unique story to live and our own way of creating that story. I also realized that ingrained habits and beliefs, like emotions, were neither good nor bad and could either hurt or enlighten. Similarly, while my many human skins, from athlete and college student to businesswoman and yoga teacher, had served my growth, none was meant to hold me for a lifetime. Rather than seeing human skins as things to cling to or run from, I suddenly saw them as mediums through which souls can experience their many facets, each one as transient as a comet flying through space.

As for the Great Truth, I now knew much more. The Great Truth never falls apart or disappears when you hold it in your hands. It is not tricky or hidden. It is not given to some and denied to others. It never makes you feel less than, better than, or separate from anyone else. The Great Truth doesn't judge or condemn. Instead, the Great Truth empowers, and is inclusive, loving, unconditional, free, and always available. It opens the doors to curiosity and enthusiasm for life. It brings us into full awareness of our humanness and our remembered divinity. It frees us to be authentic and share who we are, which is the only human offering that truly matters. And hunting for it—in many unique human skins with their individual beginnings, endings, and new beginnings—has been the greatest joy of my life.

# ABOUT THE AUTHOR

ON THE SURFACE, KERI MANGIS might seem a candid yet introverted observer of life. But peel back a layer and you'll uncover an inquisitive explorer of internal and external realms. Peel back another layer and you might see a brave visionary pioneering her own brand of spiritual revolution. She has studied yoga, Ayurveda, herbal medicine, energy work, aromatherapy, Buddhism, Hinduism, Tantra, Christianity, and other spiritual teachings and healing modalities that have sparked her endless curiosity. She is currently a freelance writer and speaker whose work has appeared in *Elephant Journal, The Urban Howl, The Sunlight Press, Grown and Flown, Rebelle Society, The Good Men Project, Stitch, Literary Mama*, and other publications. *Embodying Soul* is her first book. To find more of her writing, visit www.kerimangis.com.